R20038646I4

W9-BWA-518

The Golden Lad

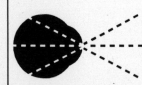

This Large Print Book carries the
Seal of Approval of N.A.V.H.

THE GOLDEN LAD

THE HAUNTING STORY OF QUENTIN AND THEODORE ROOSEVELT

ERIC BURNS

THORNDIKE PRESS

A part of Gale, Cengage Learning

GALE
CENGAGE Learning·

Farmington Hills, Mich • San Francisco • New York • Waterville, Maine
Meriden, Conn • Mason, Ohio • Chicago

GALE
CENGAGE Learning·

LIBRARY OF CONGRESS CATALOGING-IN-PUBLICATION DATA

Names: Burns, Eric, author.
Title: The golden lad : the haunting story of Quentin and Theodore Roosevelt / by Eric Burns.
Description: Large print edition. | Waterville : Thorndike Press, 2016. | Series: Thorndike Press large print biographies and memoirs
Identifiers: LCCN 2016004001 | ISBN 9781410490056 (hardcover) | ISBN 141049005X (hardcover) | Includes bibliographical references.
Subjects: LCSH: Roosevelt, Quentin, 1897–1918. | Roosevelt, Theodore, 1858–1919—Family. | Children of presidents—United States—Biography. | Fighter pilots—United States—Biography. | United States. Army. Air Service. Aero Squadron, 95th. | Fathers and sons—United States—Biography.
Classification: LCC E757.3 .B87 2016 | DDC 973.91/10922—dc23
LC record available at http://lccn.loc.gov/2016004001

Published in 2016 by arrangement with Pegasus Books, LLC

Printed in Mexico
1 2 3 4 5 6 7 20 19 18 17 16

Theodore Roosevelt, the most bellicose man ever to serve as President of the United States, a believer in war as good exercise for a nation.

Quentin Roosevelt, Theodore's youngest and favorite son, not so bellicose, but ready to make his father proud by taking to the air in World War I.

THIS BOOK IS DEDICATED TO

John Fontanella
209 Russell Hall
Westminster College
New Wilmington, Pennsylvania 16142

To this day the peer I admire most

CONTENTS

PREFACE:
THE GRAND DREAM
OF A LITTLE BOY

There were times when the boy thought of death. Not so unusual, really. And not so morbid. After all, death is life's biggest mystery, and bright children like Teedie are inherently curious. They try to imagine the void, the end of all sensations, but cannot do it. No one can, especially those who have spent so little time being alive. But what Teedie *could* imagine was how he wanted his own sensations to end. He wanted to die in war, he decided at an early age — a glorious death at a glorious moment for a glorious cause on a battlefield that historians would long remember. Since a person *had* to die, Teedie decided, there was no better means of entering the realm of eternal darkness than to be struck by an enemy's bullet, especially after having struck a number of enemies first.

It all seemed so glorious. Then again, he was just a boy.

11

ONE:
THE BEGINNING OF THE STORY

1

It was 1897, it was time. Actually, for Theodore Roosevelt it was past time. He wanted the Spanish-American War to begin. He wanted *any* war to begin. He believed in war. It was like eating the right foods, getting enough rest, enough exercise. Yes, that most of all: exercise — and Roosevelt more than most people knew the value of exercise. "No national life is worth having," he said, in one of his many encomiums to combat, "if the nation is not willing, when the need shall arise, to stake everything on the supreme arbitrament of war, and to pour out its blood, its treasures, its tears like water rather than to submit to the loss of honor and renown."

The *Washington Post* "was charmed with such manly sentiments," responding the next day with a warm, editorial round of applause. "Well done, nobly spoken!" the paper raved. "Theodore Roosevelt, you have found your proper place at last — all hail!"

But all did *not* hail. All did not realize, as Roosevelt did, that you could learn a lot about a person from his attitude toward war, that it was "a supreme test of a man's character." Nor did all realize that you could learn a lot about a nation, as war provided "a way for society to work together for common ideals." He was troubled that so many people did not understand, that they were timid, unresponsive to challenge, that their "cult is nonvirility."

Roosevelt justified war in a number of ways, among them as a glorious expression of righteousness. To many of his countrymen, this was the most disturbing of his rationales. Not only could they not see a connection between war and righteousness, they believed that one was the opposite of the other. So many people refuting Theodore Roosevelt when he explained so just a cause. It made no sense to him. It was, he supposed, something he would just have to live with. But could his nation live with it?

His trigger finger was itchy long before the Spanish-American War was even a glint in America's eye.

In 1886, then a New York State assemblyman about to finish third in his bid for the governorship, Roosevelt wrote to Secretary of War William C. Endicott "offering to try to raise some companies of horse riflemen . . . in the event of trouble with Mexico." But there was no trouble with Mexico, not yet, and the offer seemed to have no purpose other than to encourage it.

And near the turn of the century, writing the third of his four-volume history, *The Winning of the West,* he worked himself into a froth over the very first Americans. In the chapter titled "The Indian Wars," he belittled the notion of civilized discourse with native tribes. "[L]ooked at from the standpoint of the ultimate result," he stated, "there was little real difference to the Indian whether the land was taken by treaty or by war." The Colt Peacemaker, the Winchester, the breech-loader, and the rifled musket — these, Roosevelt determined, were the appropriate means of dealing with primitive peoples. Then, concluding: "The most ultimately righteous of all wars is a war with savages, though it is apt to be also the most terrible and inhuman. The rude, fierce settler who drives the savage from the land lays all civilized mankind under a debt to him."

But when he finished writing, he continued fuming about his being trapped in a

15

time of peace. There was a dispute between the United States and England about territorial rights in South America, specifically about the border between British Guiana and Venezuela. Roosevelt thought the countries should stop arguing and start fighting. But who, other than Theodore Roosevelt, would advocate war over an inconsequential border tiff in South America that did not involve the United States in the first place! No matter. Theodore vented by writing a letter to newspapers criticizing "the Baboo kind of statesmanship . . . which is clamored for at this moment by the men who put monetary gain before national honor, or who are still intellectually in a state of colonial dependence on England."

No one knew what Baboo statesmanship was; no one even knew what a Baboo was. But just the sound was enough: no statesman wanted to be thought of as Baboo-ish in his outlook.

Theodore Roosevelt, with pen in hand, the grip firmer than necessary, as if it were a weapon he held, and thrust with each word.

2

On November nineteenth, 1897, there was something that demanded Roosevelt's attention more than the absence of battle, of carnage and strife, of gunfire and bayonets. In the midst of a few days off from his position as Assistant Secretary of the Navy, he stood in his study and looked out on the grounds of his Sagamore Hill Estate, which sat atop a slight rise in the Long Island, New York village of Oyster Bay. For a few minutes, he tried not to listen to the noisy anguish above him. It was impossible. Yielding to it, he would climb the stairs again and stand in the hallway outside the door to his wife's room, calling her name, willing her to be a trouper, urging her through her pain. He had done it before. So had she, four times previously.

It was a colder day than usual for the season. The lawn had taken on its late-autumn coat of washed-out green, ending at an enormous field of daisies, the delight of all the Roosevelts in spring and summer, but now a jumble of shivering stalks that looked as if they would not survive until warm weather could allow them to bloom again. Behind them was a wooded area of bare-limbed trees: maples, oaks, and a single copper beech.

Not a leaf to be seen on any of them. Occasionally, in a swooping vee formation, a flock of geese would pass overhead, dipping

17

into low-hanging clouds, then appearing again in the distance. They had been suitably warned by dropping temperatures and were heading south with all due haste.

Everything was peaceful, then, at Sagamore Hill on this November day, all as it should have been, except in the bedroom where Edith Roosevelt lay, and where a child, a son to be named Quentin, was struggling to be born. His mother, her eyes red and teary, grunted, panted, grabbed on to the bedposts with white knuckles and tried to shake the posts loose, crying until she was hoarse.

Theodore had once expressed his awe and humility at the process of bringing life into the world. "The birth pangs make all men the debtors of all women," he said. And, tempting hyperbole in light of his own views, he had gone on to state, "No man, not even the soldier who does his duty, stands quite on the level of the wife and mother who has done her duty."

Finally, Edith's efforts were rewarded. The crown of the infant's head poked out of her, and the rest of her child slid behind it into the world: pink, stout, robust — and crying just as loudly as his mother.

As soon as Roosevelt heard the baby, he

18

pounded on the door and entered without invitation. He sprang to Edith's side — taking out a handkerchief and wiping her forehead, stroking her cheek with the back of his hand, cooing at her. She forced a smile back at him but could not keep it. Her eyelids fell as her lips fell as her breathing fell, albeit gradually, to a pace more closely resembling normal. Roosevelt took her hand in his and squeezed it. She did not move.

Then, as if saving the better for last, he turned and looked at his boy. He nodded, and the wet nurse handed him over, watching as the child quieted himself a little and settled into his father's embrace, so gentle for such a robust man. He rocked little Quentin back and forth in his arms. He spoke to him in nonsense syllables. He held up his thumb and wrapped the baby's tiny fingers partway around it. When he let go, the fingers stayed in place. According to Sagamore lore, something seemed to pass between father and son in that moment, and it went beyond merely a parent's joy and a newborn's motor reflexes. As was written by the picture editor Joan Paterson Kerr, "A baby's hand, [Theodore] thought, was the most beautiful of God's creations."

■ ■ ■ ■

Quentin was the sixth of the Roosevelt children, and the brood was now complete. First had come Alice, Theodore's daughter by his first wife, Alice Hathaway Lee Roosevelt, who suffered from Bright's disease, a kidney ailment that we would today refer to as nephritis. She had died an agonizing death on the same day that Roosevelt's mother had passed away. Daughter Alice not only possessed her mother's name, but her appearance, her demeanor, her mannerisms — curses, every one of them, as far as her father was concerned; he could never quite forgive young Alice for the painful memories she stirred in him. In fact, he had always suspected that "the birth pangs" caused by his daughter had contributed to the end of his beloved's life, weakening her, lessening her resistance to the disease she had needed all of her energy to fight. It is possible he was right.

With Edith, he had helped bring into the world the other five youngsters: Theodore, Jr., who followed Alice by three years in 1887 and was known as Ted, or Ted, Jr.; Kermit, born two years after Ted, who would die too young as a result of a seizure,

20

probably induced by alcohol; Ethel, appearing two years after Kermit and named for Alice Lee's mother; Archibald, called Archie, who came along after four more years had passed; and now, in 1897, Quentin, already with a grip on his father. And, apparently, on his mother as well. In the days ahead, she would find him "the merriest, jolliest baby imaginable."

Four boys and two girls in little more than a decade. The former, following two decades, and on the eve of the greatest adventure of their lives, would be known in the family as the Golden Lads.

"Very unexpectedly, Quentin Roosevelt appeared just two hours ago," Theodore wrote to his sister, having returned his son to the nurse and himself to the study, sitting in the oversized chair behind his desk. Then, after claiming that "Edith is doing well," he folded the message and summoned one of his servants. The man took the paper, dashed outside, and mounted his horse, riding the three miles from Sagamore Hill to the village drugstore, site of the only phone in Oyster Bay. The servant called Western Union, read the message to the dispatcher, and, moments later, Anna Roosevelt Cowles, nicknamed Bamie, became the first of the aunts and uncles to learn of the family's latest addition. She listened to the news with a delighted smile, then hung up, opened her private phone book, and began spreading the word along to the rest of the family. So much more fulfilling a means of communicating significance than technology has brought us today, with its buttons and beeps, its encoded emotionlessness.

But even before the servant had slipped his feet into the stirrups for the ride to the telephone, Theodore had returned his pen into the inkwell and started writing again — the first of two letters to be dispatched by regular mail. The first notified the headmaster of Groton, a prestigious prep school in Massachusetts, of Quentin's existence. It asked that, when the time came, the boy be considered for enrollment. It was only a formality. The acceptance would be, too. All Roosevelts went to Groton. The newest would not be eligible for twelve years, but Theodore wanted to ensure his son's place as soon as he knew that Quentin had been born healthy.

The second missive went to Roosevelt's underlings at the Naval Department, where he served as Assistant Secretary, and perhaps he squeezed his pen even more tightly now, as his wife had so recently done with the bedposts. He started in on another piece of stationery. "To speak with a frankness which our timid friends would call brutal," he began, "I would regard a war with Spain from two standpoints: first, the advisability on the grounds of humanity and self interest of interfering on behalf of the Cubans . . . second . . . the benefit done our military forces *by trying both the Navy and Army in actual practice. . . .*"

And so the contradiction that both fueled Theodore's life and shortened it, his love of Sagamore Hill, because in it were housed "all things beautiful . . . rifles and children."

3

Edith Kermit Carow Roosevelt did not emerge from childbirth well, as her husband had written, certainly not as well as her child. Quentin slept soundly, drank deeply whenever the breast was offered, and pounded his mattress with his hands and feet at times when he felt an excess of vigor, which was most of his waking hours. Theodore would look down at his son at moments like this and smile — all that energy! Just like his father, thought the nurses and other household help who had been around long enough to remember.

Edith, however, remained bedridden long

after the nurse and nanny took charge of the boy, long after the first snowfall covered the lawns at Sagamore Hill, the crust of ice atop it as shiny as if the Roosevelts had instructed their servants to polish it for company. The tree limbs had begun to bend under the weight of the snow, and the daisy stalks were buried now, invisible to the eye. Also invisible, except for a few faint tracks from horses and carriages, was the driveway leading to the main entrance of the manse.

Inside, Quentin's mother lay on her back, her forehead aflame. For more than a month her temperature never dropped below 101. Her entire body ached, including her eyes; she could neither read nor write, except for sending off an occasional postcard about the arrival of her little boy. Several doctors were summoned. Each prescribed a different treatment. None of them worked.

Throughout the rest of November and into December, Edith kept to her room. She seemed to improve late in December, shortly after Christmas, but took a turn for the worse in January. Archie, and of course Quentin, were too young to understand what was happening. But Alice, Ted, Ethel, and Kermit knew that their mother was sick, sicker than she was supposed to be after having had a baby, and they were wor-

24

ried. From the bedrooms of the latter three, it was not uncommon to hear sniffles at bedtime.

As for Theodore, he could not help but fear that he would lose another wife to childbirth. The sensation haunted him, and when he gave in to it he could actually feel a quivering inside. He had to do something, for his sake, for both of their sakes. Midway through January, believing he could afford no more time away from the Navy Department, he returned to Washington. Edith made the trip with him, tucked into her train car as comfortably as could be, with a physician and nurses attending to her every need. But she undertook the journey not so much because Theodore needed her presence as because he believed she would receive better medical care in the nation's capital. Eventually, she would.

But, as genuinely as Roosevelt empathized with his wife, what is not certain is how deep the feeling went. It was not that Theodore was an uncaring man; he was, rather, an unfortunate one.

On the day that his first wife and mother had died, February 14, 1884, the Feast of St. Valentine's, the two of them were in the same New York townhouse, one floor away from each other. As time ran out on each of

25

them, Theodore spent hour after hour running from one bedroom to another, up the stairs and down, up and down, panting and occasionally stumbling as he did everything he could for the two women dearest to him — which turned out to be nothing. It might have been comical, a scene from a Mack Sennett short, to one who did not know what drove Theodore so frantically.

His mother died first. After Alice passed away, eleven hours later, Theodore withdrew to his office, collapsed into his chair, and scratched a thick, black "X" in his diary. He wrote, "The light has gone out of my life."

And so one concludes: a person who has undergone so profound a tragedy becomes more sensitive to the travails of others. He knows their torment, feels it himself. He cannot help it; his heart begins to ache without conscious effort, even though in reality the distress belongs to those other than him.

That is one possibility. But there is another. At times, the opposite reaction occurs. Having fought his way through his own miseries, a man cannot be as patient as he would like to be for the misfortunes of others, even those for whom he cares most. He survived; so should they. Once it had been his turn to suffer, now it was theirs. It seems a cold-hearted description of a man's emotional state, but that does not make it untrue. Nor does it imply that it is the only emotional state of which a man is capable, or even the predominant one at a time of crisis. But it does explain, perhaps as well as possible, why a man who loves — and empathizes — can simultaneously roil inside as the object of his affection struggles for recovery. Especially in this case. Edith had given birth so easily to her previous four children; why had the fifth led to such ongoing misery? Roosevelt might have been sensitive to birth pangs, but that did not mean he — or any other man, for that matter — understood them.

4

The Spanish-American war was fought neither in Spain nor in America. Rather, the battles raged in Guam, Puerto Rico, the Philippines, and, most of all, Cuba. As they drew ever closer, Roosevelt could almost see himself in uniform, almost feel the stock of the rifle nestled into his shoulder, the kick of the recoil when he fired. He could not have been more impatient for his dreams to come true.

But Edith would not cooperate, would not put him at ease for his departure. *Could* not

27

put him at ease. Showing no signs of improvement, she not only became weaker by the day but sometimes less coherent.

Finally, after having denied permission for her to be operated on in February, Roosevelt, who had already sought a variety of medical opinions, sought one more, this time from someone other than "a lot of perfectly incompetent doctors, taxidermists and veterinarians."

The perfectly competent doctor upon whom Roosevelt now decided to rely, and who noted the swelling in Edith's abdomen, was Sir William Osler, a Canadian on the faculty of Johns Hopkins University in Baltimore.

Examining Theodore's wife, he was immediately alarmed, declaring that Edith would have to be operated on as soon as possible. But the prospect of surgery was a fearful one. She turned to her husband, standing next to Sir William, who had already begun his preparations, summoning assistance. Theodore nodded, lips pursed in determination, and then dropped to her bedside, "holding her hand until ether removed her from him."

The procedure, performed early in March, "revealed an abscess near the hip, and was completely successful." When Roosevelt heard the news, he clapped his hands together and positively beamed. He tramped up and down the corridors of the hospital with his head bobbing in relief. Later, he would praise Edith for behaving "heroically; quiet and even laughing, while I held her hand until the ghastly preparations had been made." But "it was a severe operation, and her convalescence may be a matter of months," Roosevelt admitted. Nonetheless, he told one and all, "she is crawling back to life," and he could not have been more proud of her.

Four months later, though, his wife was still not her normal self. Her "squarish face" was no longer so wan, her "strong jaw" no longer so slack, and she had regained the "handsomeness that suited her sober personality." But she had regained only a portion of her previous strength and continued to rely on servants for virtually all household duties. She was seldom in pain any longer, but her steps were sometimes unsteady and at other times her speech did not sound as crisp as usual. For the most part, all she wanted to do was rest.

Still, she was on the road to becoming herself again, and with her youngest son already beginning to develop that extraordinary personality of his, entertaining his mother as if to make amends for all the suffering he had caused, Theodore decided it was time to take a road of his own. He told her he could wait no longer. The battle was beginning; he must be off. Edith smiled and nodded at him. She told him to go. He told her how much it meant to him that she understood. He was already packed.

Shortly afterward, he cabled a fellow man-at-arms who had just arrived at the final way station before Cuba. "Do not make peace until we get to Porto Rico [*sic*]." He wanted the war, which had just begun, to wait for him, and it did. A few weeks later, he would inspire a band of men to victory, storming up one of the two hills in Cuba known as the San Juan Heights. He would wave his sword at the bullets whizzing past his head as if it were a magic wand; he would cajole his men, demanding their obedience, and, to all appearances, would be having the time of his life. And, although he had no way of knowing it then, tiny Quentin's father would become, as the leader of the Rough Riders, an icon like no other of his era.

Two:
The Heart of the Story

1

How, though, does one become a national icon, a name known to all, a face on Mount Rushmore? Surely not just by immersing himself in books as a child. But for young Teedie, as he was known in the family, literature was a passion. Among other volumes, he read the adventure tales of James Fenimore Cooper, Captain Frederick Marryat's *Mr. Midshipman Easy,* and Longfellow's *Saga of King Olaf,* an epic poem of bloodshed and revenge, which he is said to have memorized.

Teedie "found the first, island-bound part of *Robinson Crusoe* tame; the second part, where the hero takes on the wolves of the Pyrenees and wanders about the Far East, was much more to his taste." As was *The Scalp Hunters,* in which the title body part is an item of commerce; and *Under Two Flags,* a tale of the Honorable Bertie Cecil, an Englishman who exiles himself to Algeria and joins a fighting corps of men from a variety of nations known as the *Chasseurs d'Afrique.*

As far as magazines were concerned, Teedie's favorite was *Our Young Folks,* which taught boys "manliness, decency and good conduct."

Eventually, with the help of a tutor, he learned to read French, German, and Latin. As was the custom with children in Rooseveltian society, which was probably the second tier of the upper class, Teedie was educated at home for what we today call the elementary school years, and often beyond. He was a remarkably bright boy, a citizen of a broad world of learning. But even he knew that learning took up too much of his time, that he spent too many hours sitting at a desk or stretched out on the sofa, book in hand, notebook and pen at the ready.

There was little, though, that he could do about it. For the most part, his inactivity was forced on him. He was the frailest member of a family that, despite public perception, was itself almost unanimously frail. He suffered from headaches, fevers, stomach pains, diarrhea, gastrointestinal ailments, "and as many other maladies as he had names for."

His most severe problems, however, were the result of asthma. "First appearing not long after he learned to talk, it recurrently seized the child by the bronchi and nearly suffocated him." The attacks came at unpredictable times and lasted for unpredictable intervals — from minutes to hours to most of a day. "They were terrifying; try as he might to breathe, he couldn't get enough air. He gasped and wheezed and choked, not knowing whether each frantic gasp might be his last." During his worst attacks, Teedie could not summon enough breath to blow out the candle at his bedside.

Not in the least did he resemble his heroes of fiction.

Years later, he would look back on his childhood sufferings and conclude that they would have a permanent effect on his health. He would die, he told friends, at age sixty. He was exactly right: he was born in October 1858 and died in January 1919, so he had not yet had his sixty-first birthday.

Teedie's father was troubled about his son, but he knew what to do. The elder Roosevelt always knew what to do. "He not only took great and untiring care of me," Theodore would in time say, and then point out that

33

"some of my early remembrances are of nights when he would walk up and down with me for an hour at a time in his arms when I was a wretched mite suffering acutely from asthma — but he also refused to coddle me, and made me feel that I must force myself to hold my own with other boys and prepare to do the rough work of the world."

Theodore Roosevelt, Senior. A successful and socially connected businessman, an importer of plate glass, an investor in real estate, a banker — but a man who valued integrity no less than dollars, and thus, given the venal examples of the robber barons who dominated the press and the conversation of the times, was more admired than emulated. To his son, Theodore Senior provided advice that would become "the most enduring and potent piece of the Roosevelt legend." He told Teedie he must begin a regimen of strenuous physical activity, and that whenever possible he should do his exercising outdoors, so the sun could beat down on him and the occasional breezes of lower Manhattan could invigorate him as the sweat dried on his skin and he struggled to fill his lungs with every last molecule of oxygen they could hold. At the start, he coughed most of them out.

When the weather forced him inside, Teedie was able to exercise in a small gym that his father had built for him in a corner of their home, one that included Indian clubs and rings attached to the ceiling and weights of all poundage, size, and function.

"Theodore," he told his boy, "you have the mind, but you have not the body, and without the help of the body the mind cannot go as far as it should. You must make your body." Theodore Senior paused for a moment, allowing the words to sink in. Then, continuing: "It is hard drudgery to make one's body, but I know you will do it."

Teedie was not nearly as confident. In the days that followed, there were moments when his father's counsel seemed a means of further torment rather than a cure. Asthma *and* exercise? But there were also moments of trust, moments when the boy gave himself up to his father's reassuring and steadfast presence, his carefully chosen words, and felt the peace that comes with determination.

"I'll make my body," he vowed, and his word was as good in this case as Theodore Senior's was in business.

The elder Roosevelt was more than his son's sire; he was his idol. As a boy, Teedie "began applying to others the code of behavior he learned from his father. A fellow must avoid profanity, [and] excessive drinking, and maintain a high standard of personal ethics. Yet, at the same time, he must show proof of his virility in other ways to retain the respect of his fellows."

Once he reached manhood, and his father was gone, Theodore, who was not called Junior, and was only seldom referred to by his friends as Teddy, did not make a decision without asking himself what Senior would have done in a similar situation — or so his family believed. Even upon achieving the highest office in the land, he called upon his father at times of indecision. His father could not reply, of course, not in any conventional manner, but the habit had become so deeply ingrained that Theodore sought his advice regardless. And, more often than not, acted as if he had received it. The son would never allow the father to depart.

It was in 1878 that Senior's mortal departure occurred. He was a mere forty-six years old, his son only twenty, when he died painfully of cancer. It was, Theodore told his diary, "the blackest day of my life." And, the following week, he wrote more expansively: "I felt as if I had been stunned, or as if part of my life had been taken away; and the two moments of sharp, bitter agony, when I kissed the dear, dead face and realized that he would never again on this earth speak to me or greet me with his loving smile, and then when I heard the sound of the first clod dropping on the coffin holding the one I loved dearest on earth."

Some years after that, of course, Theodore's mother and first wife would provide an even blacker day. Taken together, the three deaths made sympathy for others, even his dearest second wife Edith, something with which Roosevelt would grapple for the rest of his life. And Theodore's brother Elliott had already begun the process of self-abuse that would lead to his death. Ironically, Teedie, the young asthmatic, had grown into the family's most virile surviving member.

Only once did his father disappoint him, and Theodore Senior was well aware of the fact, for he had disappointed himself in the process. Yet what was he to do?

Teedie was not yet three years old at the time and did not know what had happened. But as he grew older and paid attention to family conversations about the decision, the story came clear to him, and it never stopped nagging. It would in time lay the groundwork for his philosophy about a citizen's debt to his country, especially regarding armed combat, and it was upon this groundwork that he would stand unyieldingly for his entire life.

During the Civil War, it had been legal for a man to avoid conscription by paying another man to take his place. But had it been ethical? The topic was debated, sometimes angrily, in the House and Senate, the tavern and church hall, the workplace and playing field. And, internally, the debate raged within Theodore Roosevelt, Senior, who believed the policy of hiring substitutes favored the well-to-do, which he most certainly was himself.

But there were extenuating circumstances. As the war broke out, he had three young children at home, a fourth on the way, and a wife in delicate health, as his son's wife Edith would one day be. How could he leave her in such circumstances? How could she manage without him?

There was yet another circumstance, this one even more vexing. Theodore Senior was not afraid of battle — no Roosevelt was or ever would be — and he was a tenacious believer in the Union cause. It was not, however, a view shared by all his family. Three of its members — his mother, sister Bamie, and wife Martha — might have lived in the North, but their sympathies, and even some of their property, lay in the South. They owned a plantation. They owned the slaves that worked the plantation. Two of Martha and Anna's brothers had donned Confederate gray for the war. And so Theodore Senior was forced to ask himself: Could he run the risk of firing upon those to whom he was related? If he did so, would his family be torn apart, the Southerners become outcasts?

Not unreasonably, he decided it would be impossible for him to serve. After much wavering, he came down on the side of being a civilian, of hiring others to do the fighting. Theodore Senior employed two men, for different periods of time, to take his place in uniform. He was not comfortable with such a plan, but could see no other way out of his dilemma.

The cost: $600, three hundred for each of the substitutes.

The cost, reckoned in different terms: unceasing self-doubt.

Teedie's father paid the former, suffered the latter. As his son would later say, his father "always afterward felt that he had done a very wrong thing."

Still, he remained the boy's hero, a man who "combined strength and courage with gentleness, tenderness, and great unselfishness." Theodore continued to depend on his wisdom, admire his rectitude, follow his example.

Except in this case. In this case, he simply could not. Even as a teenager, when the fighting was long over, Theodore knew that, if faced with the same choice, he would have taken up arms for the Union cause. Neither the repercussions to the life of his family nor the possibility of his falling victim to enemy fire would have mattered. When one is called to fight for his country, which Theodore believed — in the case of the Civil War — was synonymous with the North, one answers in the affirmative and lets the chips fall where they may. Or so he said. It must be kept in mind that he never personally faced such a choice.

So — verbally, at least — he kept to his position for the rest of his life. Long after his teenage years, in a letter to the British author Rudyard Kipling, a man of martial outlook as pronounced as his own, Roosevelt wrote of how he raised his children. "I have always explained to my four sons that, if there is a war during their lifetime, I wish them to be in a position to explain to their children why they did go to it, and not why they did not go to it."

Theodore Senior had taken a different position. Tellingly, his son did not refer to it in his autobiography, nor did he even refer to his father's death. He did not mention his mother's death of typhoid fever at the age of forty-eight. He did not reveal that she had died on the same day that his first wife passed away, a mere twenty-two years old; in fact, he did not acknowledge Alice at all, as if Edith were the first and only woman to have won his heart. It was Theodore's way: hide the evidence, ignore the facts; if it is not part of the official record, who is to say it ever happened? Soldier on! Survive at all costs!

2

Teedie began making his body not only by working out at home, but even more by signing up at Wood's Gymnasium in New York, "where he swung chest weights with such energy that his mother wondered aloud 'how many horse-power he was expending.' " After a while he began, if not quite to enjoy pumping iron, at least to dread it less than he had at the start. And he quickly came to enjoy the results. The boy who had only months earlier been an invalid, was instead becoming the physical approximation of a man. By the end of the day he was exhausted; but with his self-imposed boot camp over, he forced himself to book camp, reading and learning until he could stay awake no longer. Then, effortlessly, he blew out the candle at his bedside.

"For many years," Corinne Roosevelt later wrote of her brother, "one of my most vivid recollections is seeing him between horizontal bars, widening his chest by regular, monotonous motion — drudgery indeed."

Teedie also ran back and forth on neighborhood streets, climbed nearby hills, ice-skated until his companions gave up in exhaustion, rowed boats, and rode horses. He even learned to handle a shotgun, one he had received as a Christmas present from his father. It was a family tradition. Thanks to lessons from Teedie as a grown man, son Ted had killed a buck when he was fourteen and a moose at seventeen. Before he was twenty, Kermit had felled a lion and an elephant. And probably at the age of ten, if not younger, Teedie began roaming through the woods close to Sagamore and firing away at birds of all sorts, everything he could see that flew. One morning, or so he claimed, "he found he could bring down five starlings with a single shot."

He missed more often than he hit, much more. But when fortunate enough to achieve the latter result, Teedie scurried after his prey, retrieved them and eagerly took them home to show off. If Edith was the only family member present, the boy was unlikely to be received with the fanfare he desired. More often than not, she would demand that he dispose of the poor dead birds, and he obeyed. As time went on, though, he occasionally received permission to take the tiny carcasses to his room to study, carefully cutting them open to try to understand their internal workings, as fascinated with their anatomy as he was with his own marksmanship. After a time, he would stuff the birds, turning them into souvenirs. He might later have cursed the doctors who treated Edith after Quentin's birth as taxidermists, but as a child he took pleasure in being one himself. He kept a collection of his favorite birds atop his bookcase.

But eventually, he began to think that birds were too beautiful and frail to be gunned down. Teedie stopped shooting them and concentrated instead on research, reading book after book about birdwatching, and filling notebook after notebook about the various species he had seen.

43

In the woods now, he would satisfy himself simply by spotting them above him and recording the make and model — a sniper no longer.

But not all of his activities were peaceful. After his bird-watching days ended, Teedie made a drastic change to the boxing ring, developing a fascination with the sport that would last well into adulthood. At Harvard, twenty-one years of age, he fought for the school's lightweight boxing championship, losing when his opponent landed a punch after the bell. In following years, he put on a pair of gloves and tried to pound a foe into submission whenever he could. He did not think so much in terms of pain, either suffered or inflicted; rather, he thought in terms of victory, validation of self.

Roosevelt even entered the ring from time to time in the White House — until, that is, he was pounded into submission himself. It happened when "a young artillery captain smashed enough blood vessels in his left eye to cause permanent dimness. Ultimately, he lost all sight in that eye. He had the consideration to make sure that the officer's name was never made public."

Nonetheless, the officer was horrified. He had severely wounded the President of the United States! That Roosevelt kept his name and deed a secret struck the young man as an act of extraordinary kindness; he was forever grateful. To his victim, however, it was simply a matter of acting as a sportsman was compelled to act.

The process was arduous, this making of the body, but Teedie was accomplishing it: overcoming his asthma, ridding himself of stomach aches, seldom running a fever anymore. He felt like a different person, and his father was generous in dispensing praise.

But it may be that no one admired Teedie's transformation more than his younger brother Elliott. At the same time, it is possible that no one resented it more. The relationship between the boy and his sibling was not a conventional one. Teedie loved his brother, who was usually a loving child in return, the two of them almost equally playful and caring. But there were other times when Elliott's behavior was a puzzle to Teedie; it was as if his brother were angry at him, although there never seemed to be a reason. Elliott could be moody and mercurial to a degree that Teedie had never encountered with any other members of the family. It would be many years before he learned the reason: that Elliott, since his earliest days, had been cursed by epilepsy

45

and, worse, depression. As a result, he would later begin to rely on alcohol — and the more he imbibed, the deeper he sank into his woes.

Ultimately, the bottle could not save him. It had, in fact, the opposite effect. In 1894, at the age of thirty-four, a few days after his alcohol-fueled depression had led him to a suicide attempt by jumping out a window, Elliott fell victim to a fatal seizure. Theodore was saddened yet again; but, however much he hurt, his brother's death was but further tragedy for Roosevelt to ignore in his biography: his father, his mother, his wife Alice, and now sibling Elliott — all of them gone to their eternal rewards without Theodore's literary acknowledgment. And he, encircled by all this death, was himself a mere thirty-six. Surely he realized, as Elliott was lowered into the ground, that by his own reckoning he had only twenty-four years left to himself.

As a result of his body-building program, Teedie had in a matter of years turned himself unmistakably into Theodore. To those who had not seen him for a while, the change was startling. He still wore his thick glasses, and would in fact always wear them, but the young man was barrel-chested now instead of reed-like; his arms were well-muscled instead of splintery; and his legs fairly bulged under his trousers rather than running down from his hips like a couple of barrel-slats loosely attached. His face had not yet filled out, but it was beginning to assume its characteristic and hearty ovalness, and as it did he began to smile more, showing a large mouthful of teeth.

Or was it a mouthful of large teeth? Regardless, they would later become a caricaturist's delight. In 1895, while serving as the Police Commissioner of New York and sometimes making midnight raids to check on the behavior of his subordinates, it was said that "[t]he flash of his teeth in the night was enough to scare the most corrupt copper back to good behavior." And if that corrupt copper wasn't scared and decided to challenge his boss with fisticuffs, Theodore was more than ready.

He had kept his promise to his father. He had "made his body," even dentally.

3

Accompanying his physical changes was an inevitable change in Theodore's world view. It was, perhaps, inevitable. A person who worked as hard in childhood as Roosevelt did would find the experiences formative and the implications life-altering. In simple terms, his thinking seems to have progressed as follows: Weakness is a danger. Strength provides protection. The greater the strength, the greater the number of dangers that can be thwarted. Ultimately, strength becomes a virtue in itself, and one begins to seek outlets to express it — for the sheer joy of exertion, the pleasure of feeling muscles ripple, whether there is just cause for these outlets or not.

Theodore Roosevelt's body-making program as a child, then, joined with his father's purchase of Civil War substitutes to become the basis of his foreign policy as an adult. Each curling of the dumbbell brought him closer to his eventual eagerness to defend the United States or rescue another nation deserving survival but lacking firepower. Each firing of his rifle at a bird made him, in time, more capable of seeing provocation in the actions of another country where none was intended. Each hook or jab landed on the jaw of a fellow pugilist eventually led to his desire to attack a nation that he perceived as hostile, and to enlist every man capable of firing a gun to be part of the attacking force. It is almost as easy to explain as that. Complex matters sometimes are. Strength unused, after all, is strength wasted.

By the eve of the Spanish-American War, Theodore had long since gone from weakling to he-man. Time for the United States to do the same. It was a sentiment he expressed, although in less personal language, in what has been called "the first great speech of his career." As the Assistant Secretary of the Navy, he chose as the site for his address the welcoming venue of the Naval War College in Newport, Rhode Island.

"All the great masterful races," he told his corps of eager listeners on June 2, 1897, "have been fighting races; and the minute that a race loses the hard fighting virtues, then . . . it has lost its proud right to stand as the equal of the best."

Later in his talk, he emphasized the point differently: "No triumph of peace is quite so great as the supreme triumphs of war. . . . It may be that at some time in the dim future of the race the need for war will vanish; but that time is yet ages distant. As yet no nation can hold its place in the world, or can do any work really worth doing, unless it stands ready to guard its rights with an armed hand."

The ovation that greeted his remarks,

although to be expected given the audience, was deafening.

4

For many years, Cuba had been ruled by Spain, which treated it with dictatorial ruthlessness. To make matters worse, in 1895, the island was racked by economic depression — the forces of the marketplace collaborating with the forces of the Spanish military to make life on the island more unlivable for the natives than ever before. Some Cubans formed an army to try to overthrow the enemy, and were more successful than their foes had anticipated. They won some battles, took back some land, held their own here and there. But they were too few in number to accomplish their grander goal of self-rule. They were even too few to hold on to the land they had recaptured. They were too resolute, however, to give up the attempt. So the fighting went on, futilely; so did the Spanish oppression, ruthlessly. The island existed in a kind of menacing stasis.

Meanwhile, in the United States, interest in the conflict was growing. Fed by the imperialist impulses of Manifest Destiny, Americans wanted Cuba and other Spanish possessions such as the Philippines for their own. Fed by the wariness of long-range Spanish intentions, Americans wanted a potentially belligerent foreign power to remove itself from a base only ninety miles from U.S. shores. And fed by genuine humanitarian impulses, Americans wanted less vicious treatment of the Cubans by their occupiers. In fact, they wanted to end the occupation altogether. At one point, 400,000 Cubans were held in detention camps in and around Havana. According to some reports, half of them eventually died, the majority of starvation.

On January 25, 1898, President William McKinley took action of a sort. He dispatched the battleship U.S.S. *Maine* to Havana Harbor, not as an instrument of war, but as one of intimidation; the *Maine* was simply to sit in Cuban waters and look foreboding, a visible reminder to Spain that its ways must be mended or retribution would follow. And for three weeks the ship did just that, its intimidating bulk softly riding the waves as the crew engaged in limited duties and virtually unlimited forms of idleness.

Then came February 15. Another typical day of Caribbean winter, it seemed — sunny and warm, languid and quiet. Until, that is, the *Maine* exploded, shattering the tranquility by blowing up and disappearing, bit by bit, into a huge cloud of smoke and flames. By the time the cloud had dispersed, and the pieces of what had once been the *Maine* had plunged to the bottom of the bay, two hundred sixty-six men were dead. Another eight sailors lost their lives later due to injuries.

History has concluded that the explosion was probably an accident, that the *Maine* was obliterated by a mine which, in turn, caused the ship's forward magazines to blow up. There was never any evidence that the Spanish had placed the mine in Havana's harbor; it had, in fact, probably been there for years, perhaps set afloat by Cubans meaning to protect their island.

But given the timing, America's verdict was that the Spaniards had blown up the ship deliberately, and the suspicion was not unreasonable. Both houses of Congress urged McKinley to study the matter without delay. However, William Randolph Hearst's *New York Journal* and Joseph Pulitzer's *New York World,* competing frantically and often unethically against each other to be the country's most popular newspaper, did not urge anyone to study the matter without delay: the journalists did not study it at all. Immediately concluding that the Spaniards had destroyed the U.S. battleship, they demanded that the American military load its guns and board its battleships and take revenge without delay. Big type, bigger type; black ink, blacker ink. There is no doubt that the coverage by the two papers stirred the populace, and no doubt that the populace influenced legislators. A circulation war turned out to be one of the factors in a military war, which the United States declared on April 25.

5

No one knows who gave the First United States Volunteer Cavalry its nickname. But the Rough Riders they were called, and the Rough Riders they became to history. Theodore Roosevelt, assigned the rank of Colonel, found the appellation dashingly appropriate, appropriately self-serving. Yes, *Colonel* Roosevelt, at last a military title for a man who was at last sanctioned for military duty.

It would be the first time Theodore had ever undergone training for war, and to say that he found his performance satisfactory is to understate greatly. "I have been both astonished and pleased at my own ability in the line of tactics," he wrote. "I thoroughly enjoy handling these men, and I get them on the jump so that they can execute their movements at a gallop."

With the preliminaries over, the Rough Riders joined other American fighting men being shipped out to Cuba. As ever, even at a time like this, Roosevelt's mind was on his children. To his daughter Ethel, he sent a letter he barely had time to finish. "We are near shore now and everything is in a bustle, for we may have to disembark tonight, and I do not know when I shall have another chance to write to my . . . blessed children, whose little notes please me so. This is only a line to tell you all how much father loves you."

No less was his mind on the newest addition to the family, who had entered the world seven months ago, grasping his father's thumb.

The charge up San Juan Hill was, of course, the deed for which the Rough Riders were best known; but, officially, it never happened. The journalists got it wrong. Even some of the soldiers got it wrong. The truth is that there were two hills next to each other near the city of Santiago in an area known as the San Juan Heights. The rise that the Rough Riders surmounted was actually Kettle Hill, immediately adjacent to San Juan Hill, the latter of which played a less significant role in the war.

On July 1, Roosevelt and his men stood at the base of Kettle Hill and looked up. Their rifles were loaded and the day was perfect, "a very lovely morning," Roosevelt would one day write, "the sky of cloudless blue, while the level, shimmering rays from the just-risen sun brought into fine relief the splendid palms which here and there towered above the lower growth. The lofty and beautiful mountains hemmed in the Santiago plain, making it an amphitheatre for the battle."

It was as if he were setting out on a picnic, his path dictated by the flowery prose of a travel guide.

Yet atop Kettle Hill, the Rough Riders knew, were scores of Spanish soldiers brandishing German Mausers, a far more accurate and powerful weapon than the antiquated arms with which Roosevelt's men had been supplied. At first, learning of the disadvantage with which his men would go into battle, Roosevelt was furious, finding it evidence that his country was not prepared for even the most minor of conflicts, had not yet transformed itself from weakling to he-man, or even made the decision to do so. In fact, in his autobiography, Roosevelt berated the Spanish-American conflict as "The War of America the Unready."

Then, for self-preservation if no other reason, he changed his mind. Or, rather, his attitude. No, the United States was not properly equipped to confront its enemy, even though the need for preparation had been obvious for months; but, ever the optimist, Roosevelt found himself invigorated, rather than depressed, by the challenge. It wasn't the guns that mattered, the Colonel decided; it was the men wielding them. And, of course, the man leading those men. He had been ready for such a task, he believed, ever since he made his body. He would prove it even if he had been dispatched to Cuba with popguns.

Roosevelt mounted his horse under that cloudless blue sky and ordered his men to follow him toward the Spanish hilltop encampment. "Some responded with alacrity; others required convincing. To one trooper who was slow to rise and join the assault, Roosevelt shouted indignantly, 'Are you afraid to stand up when I am on horseback?' Stung, the man just had time to get to his feet before a bullet bored him from front to back and he fell down dead."

Roosevelt gave him but a glance. There was no time for regret. It was war, after all, and this was the kind of thing that happened.

The Rough Riders, a group of volunteers who had never been in combat before, having enlisted specifically for this engagement, were accompanied by a force of U.S. Army regulars, veterans of pale skin, as well as a black regiment, referred to by some as the "smoked Yankees." The mass of them made their way slowly but surely up Kettle Hill, firing almost indiscriminately as they climbed, "all in the spirit of the thing," Roosevelt said, "and greatly excited by the charge, the men cheering and running forward between shots." He looked around, saw "the delighted faces of the foremost officers." He knew even then that those faces "will always stay in my mind."

His own face might have been the most delighted of all. *Dee-lighted!* he would say. And when he was struck in the leg by a piece of shrapnel and stumbled for a moment, he did not lose his enthusiasm, never even grimaced. In fact, he picked up his pace all the more and kept firing. When, near the top of the hill, he dismounted, he walked with a lopsided gait but would not allow himself to be slowed by it.

Roosevelt was one of the first American soldiers to reach the summit of Kettle Hill, and he arrived to find that most of the Spaniards previously perched there had either fled or given up their lives. The surviving U.S. troops, among whom casualties were few, joined Roosevelt shortly after he completed his ascent, and they rejoiced in sloppy unison, shouting out their praises, singing the anthem and other songs of their country. They had captured the promontory. It was the major objective of the war for them, and they had achieved it. The Spaniards had the Mausers; the Americans had the will.

What they did not know was that the bloodshed was not yet over.

6

Meanwhile, Quentin, who could not keep still, such a restless child, was probably continuing his endless explorations of Sagamore Hill. On July 1, 1898, the day of his father's triumph some 1,400 miles away, the infant was at some point surely crawling toward Theodore's study. After all, it was a daily destination when the big man was there, and Quentin had no way of knowing he wasn't.

Located at the front of the house, first door on the right upon entering, the room was a dark Victorian chamber. The heavy curtains, usually drawn in Roosevelt's absence, insulated more than decorated, blocking out the cold air of winter and the steaming summer sun. And in all seasons, blocking out the light, making the study into a kind of cavern.

Over the doorway a large deer's head, with antlered headdress, stood sentry, a sense of peril to its immobility. The room where Theodore Roosevelt worked, even a room full of such benign objects as books and stationery and writing implements, was not a place for the faint of heart.

Inside the room were the mounted heads of a mountain goat, a warthog, and an antelope. Quentin probably made his way beneath them on July 1, perhaps sensing that something was wrong. He crossed a Persian carpet that covered most of the library floor. Carefully arranged on the carpet were three smaller rugs. One had formerly been the coat of a zebra and two had, in life, been the outerwear of mountain lions. Quentin would make his way over them, feeling the pleasant tickle of the animal's fur on his hands and knees, perhaps giggling, at least smiling.

But he was still puzzled.

Next, if he followed his usual path, he would circle two rocking chairs, possibly bumping into them, setting them in motion, creaking. Then he would have proceeded through the small cave under his father's desk where Theodore angled his legs while working. Where, perhaps, he had actually done some of the planning for today's military action. But he was not here now. And that was the problem for his son. Where *was* the big man, the man that Quentin, so little, was unable to call *Da-da* yet? He was usually seated in the chair that Quentin now neared. If he had been there today, Quentin would have grabbed on to one of his legs and boosted himself into a standing position. He would have waited for his father to stop working and pick him up, seating him on his lap and allowing him to lunge at the tankard of fresh roses placed daily on the desktop. But Theodore would have placed it just out of reach, petting his boy, soothing his frustration.

The child was at the stage in his development when, as much as possible, he wanted to achieve the vertical. So instead of climbing up the big man's legs, today he crawled over to the drapes and pulled himself up by grabbing handfuls of fabric, each one a little higher than the one preceding it. Standing at the drapes could not compare to standing at the big man's side, but there was no choice today.

Quentin, though, could not stand for long. After a few seconds, he would let go of the drapes and simply drop to the floor, usually in a sitting position, sometimes supine, murmuring, happy enough.

His nanny, watching it all, might step in now and pick him up. She would carry the boy to his crib, perhaps with a brief stopover at the wet nurse's breast.

What a wonderful thing to be alive, to be conscious, unbound, able to wander without purpose or restriction, except for the limitations of a tiny body! Quentin was too young to think such thoughts, of course, but he was aware of sensations — more than seven months he had been alive now, time enough to feel the joy, the freedom of movement. Seven months, and already such pleasure, so much of life, still ahead!

7

Almost as quickly as the Rough Riders' victory celebration began, it ended. Securing Kettle Hill might have been important in the long run, but all it meant at present was that the Americans had made themselves more visible to the Spaniards next door, on San Juan Hill. Theodore's men had not seen their foes at first; they were hidden behind trees, wild bushes, and rock outcroppings. Suddenly, though, with the Americans on the peak so close to them, the enemy appeared again, beginning to fire from a bewildering variety of angles — and not just with Mausers and other rifles as before, but even with a cannon they had lugged up the back side of the hill. It turned out to have been far too early for the Americans to congratulate themselves.

"At this particular time," Roosevelt later wrote, "it was trying for the men, as they were lying flat on their faces, very rarely responding to the bullets, shells, and shrapnel which swept over the hill-top, and which occasionally killed or wounded one of their number. . . .

"None of the white regulars or Rough Riders showed the slightest sign of weakening; but under the strain the colored infantry men (who had none of their officers) began to get a little uneasy and to drift to the rear. . . . This I could not allow, as it was depleting my line, so I jumped up, and walking a few yards to the rear, drew my revolver, halted the retreating soldiers, and called out to them that I appreciated the gallantry with which they had fought and would be sorry to hurt them, but that I should shoot the first man who, on any pretence whatever, went to the rear."

Thus motivated, the American troops fought back — white *and* colored, adrenaline surging through them like gasoline through one of the new automobiles back home. Their leader shouted encouragement in a constant stream, never pausing for breath. Although several of his Rough Riders were gunned down in the first volleys from San Juan Hill, Roosevelt, as strategically perceptive as he was courageous, did not worry. The issue, as he had suspected from the start, would turn out to be manpower, not firepower, and here the Americans greatly outnumbered the Spaniards. The former, continuing to defend themselves, showed no signs of surrender or even wavering. The latter, after their initial advantage, began to tire, their guns firing less often, less accurately. There were not enough cannon balls to maintain a steady barrage; there were only so many objects of such weight that the Spaniards could tote up the steep incline. Soon they retreated, slowly at first, then more and more quickly until finally their escape from the Americans was like the start of a footrace. They tucked away their weapons and sometimes stumbled over one another as they fled to lower ground for refuge from American fire.

Before long, the Spaniards had yielded the second of the adjoining hilltops. There was much more to be done in Cuba, of course, but, despite having been too congratulatory too soon, the Americans under Roosevelt's command had done their part, and done it superbly. In fact, it could be argued, having taken both of the hills when their assignment was only one, they had done more than their part.

As they watched their opponents disappear, they began to slap themselves on the back again, although warily at first. But this time, the rejoicing would endure. The Spaniards would show themselves on San Juan Heights no more. Flasks and bottles were withdrawn from backpacks and other hiding places and passed around and promptly emptied. (Some of the containers probably held a carbonated, cocaine-based soft drink called Coca-Cola, which the men had mixed with rum. A *Cuba libre,* they called it, a man's drink to celebrate a man's achievement.)

Just as the finest rum in the world was the product of Cuba, so were some of the finest grades of tobacco, which were made into the finest cigars; with these the Rough Riders were well supplied, and they followed their libations by lighting up and blowing

64

trails of smoke that drifted listlessly off toward the Caribbean sun, now beginning to sink into the horizon. Voices boomed, songs rang out. Night was approaching, and it belonged to the victors.

It is not known whether Roosevelt joined in the festivities, or, if so, to what extent. Always eager to communicate with his family, he might have spent some time with his men, then found a place of solitude where he could sit by himself and employ pen and paper. Nor is it known whether he wrote to Ted at this time; no letters to his oldest son survive. But it is likely that Ted was on his mind with the battle concluded, and, if so, the cause was likely an unfortunate one.

In the year before the war began, his father's namesake had begun to suffer from consistent headaches and "nervous prostration."

"We have been very much worried over the little fellow," Roosevelt told his sister-in-law, "for the doctors are utterly unable to find out the ultimate cause of the trouble." Eventually one physician, a family friend and likely for that reason more insightful than the others, agreed with Edith's private estimate that Ted was overwrought from trying to live up to his

65

father's excessive expectations, spoken and unspoken.

Roosevelt was embarrassed at this opinion but recognized the truth in it. He promised to go easier on the boys. . . . "Hereafter I shall never press Ted either in body or mind. The fact is that the little fellow, who is particularly dear to me, has bidden fair to be all the things I would like to have been and wasn't, and it has been a great temptation to push him."

Ted was a mere ten years old.

Whenever he could, Roosevelt wrote to his daughter Ethel, whom he had described, at birth, as "a jolly naughty whacky baby." As was the case with Quentin, there was something about Ethel that stood out, tugging at the emotions. "From an early age," it was said, "young Ethel Carow showed practical leadership qualities. Her father once remarked: 'she had a way of doing everything and managing everybody.' She quickly made her place in the family, causing upsets in her numerous fights with the sensitive Kermit. Her own sensitivity also showed. When she was four, her father was reprimanding Kermit by shaking his shoulder; Ethel, with tears in her eyes said, 'Shake me, Father.' "

And a month after the war began, with Roosevelt making final plans for the assault on Kettle Hill, he somehow found time to tell Ethel, a mere seven years old at the time and not truly aware of the dangers her father faced, that he saw a "lot of funny little lizards that run about in the duty road very fast, and then stand still with their heads up. Beautiful red cardinal birds and tanagers flit about in the woods." The content is, of course, unremarkable; the context, however, with bullets having been whizzing through the air for four weeks now, could not be more telling of the man and his love of family.

Ethel, by the way, would settle down from her infantile ways and, as a young woman, become known to some as "The Queen of Oyster Bay," and to others as "The First Lady of Oyster Bay." In fact, at perhaps one of the lowest points of her father's life, she became the Four-Star General of Sagamore Hill, and all was better because of it. No one would have believed that she had started out in life as "jolly naughty whacky."

More than anyone else, though, Theodore wrote to his wife. A short time after he and his men had cleared the San Juan Heights, he told her that "I do not want to be vain," and then, contradicting himself, continued, "but I do not think that any one else could have handled this regiment quite as I have handled it during the last three weeks." Years later, he would look back on his accomplishments in Cuba and say, "San Juan was the great day of my life."

Not long after the battle, Edith would receive a letter from one of her husband's comrades stating that her husband was "just reveling in victory and gore." It was obvious that the letter-writer was himself reveling, and thought Edith would enjoy knowing of her husband's post-battle happiness. She did not. She loved her husband, but could never make sense of his gleefully violent side. As best she could, she ignored it. It was not a wife's role to reform the man whom she had vowed before God and man to obey.

And so, in her own letters to Cuba, she kept as much as she could to the quotidian. She wanted to give Theodore the feeling that life as usual awaited him at Sagamore Hill when he finally returned, and that, in the meantime, he could rest easy about her and the children. Ted was once again healthy and enjoying his summer vacation; Ethel played with her mother's collection of old dolls and insisted that they be configured in a straight line; and Quentin was constantly on the go, amazing the family with his ability to cover so much territory so quickly on his hands and knees.

But these were not what really concerned her, were not what she felt most deeply in her heart. To her true feelings she would not yield, not in a letter to a husband at war. Except, that is, on one occasion, when she could not restrain herself any longer and confessed to him, "Always I have the longing and missing in my heart, but I shall not write about it for it makes me cry." That was all, one sentence — then she was back to her determinedly stoic self again, passing along reports of the daily routine, always putting the interests of her husband first.

The Spanish-American War, at about three months the shortest in American history, was far too brief to suit Colonel Roosevelt. And, despite his later comment about the satisfaction it gave him, he did not find it as satisfying as he would have liked. As wars went, he thought, this had not been a "great one . . . nevertheless it was a war which has decided much for our destiny and which has been of incalculable benefit to the country; a war because of which every American citizen can hold his head high, for the nation now stands as the peer of any of the Great Powers of the world, and we who fought in it hope we have proved that were are not unworthy of the men who so valiantly wore both the blue and the gray in the years from 1861 to 1865."

Roosevelt was thirty-nine years old when the war officially ended, with the United States and Spain signing a Protocol of Peace in Washington on August 12, 1898. Had he known at the time that he would never see combat again, never again command troops or fire weapons at enemy soldiers, never even map out a campaign of action from the field — that his entire length of service on the battlefield would be *three months* — he would have been demoralized, afraid that the rest of his life would be empty and pointless.

He could not have guessed the greater glories, albeit of a different nature, that awaited him.

8

By the time the protocol had been signed, Roosevelt was back at Sagamore Hill. Edith had welcomed him warmly and the children raucously. Quentin, of course, was not capable of understanding where the big man had been or what he had been doing or why.

Eventually, though, he would almost memorize the actions of his father in battle, the result of Roosevelt's telling his children about the charge up Kettle Hill night after night through their childhood years, until the stories joined those of Mother Goose, the Brothers Grimm, and other such staples of kiddy lore, becoming not merely part of the children's evening routine, but an even larger part of what they would come to stand for as adults. It was especially true for Quentin, who, when several years older, would go so far as to reenact the charge up Kettle Hill when playing with friends. On one occasion, he went *too* far.

The year was 1908. Theodore was the chief executive of the United States and Quentin, approaching eleven, was the ringleader of a band of free-spirited lads known as the White House Gang. To many who knew of their exploits, members of the Gang were nothing more than the spoiled, untamed sons of prominent Washington officials. Brats, they might have been called. To others, like the Gang's Earle Looker, thinking back on the gang as a grown man, the group that Quentin headed provided a valuable initiation, "a boy's first real encounter with his half-real world . . . he is standing upon the shadow-line of his destiny; and very soon, he must tackle reality, using much of the experience, good or bad, his association with his gang has taught him."

One day, the Gang was playing in a public room at the White House, and Quentin grabbed the sword his father had wielded in Cuba. He needed two hands to hold it, but once he got his grip, he slashed it through the air, exaggerating his father's drawl as he hollered, "Step up and see the i-d-e-n-t-i-c-a-l sword carried by Colonel Thee-a-dore Roosevelt in the capture of San Juan Hill. See it! See it!"

Or, in the case of his playmate Charles "Taffy" Taft, son of the Secretary of War and the man who would eventually succeed Roosevelt as president — Feel it! Feel it! Quentin, ignoring his parents' command never to so much as touch the sword, much less remove it from its display case, had swung it so carelessly that he sliced Taffy on the ear. Blood began to seep out immediately. Quentin was horrified. He dropped the sword and blanched, appalled at what he had done. Taffy fell to the floor, although more from surprise than anything else; the bleeding turned out to be barely a trickle. The Gang gathered around him.

Fortunately, though, Taffy was like his

father — "remarkable for his calmness, slowness to anger, good humour, and steadfast determination when roused." His pals could not help admiring him, but neither could they help fearing for themselves. What were they to do? The boys knew that at any minute an adult would come along and be much displeased. And if the adult was the President or First Lady of the entire United States. . . .

What they needed was an excuse, a cover story. It was Taffy himself, his coolness under fire only increasing, who came up with it. "Remember," he said, "I fell on a chair."

The members of the Gang looked at each other and grinned. Leave it to Taffy — who then impressed them all the more by telling them to smear some blood on the foot of the chair for verisimilitude.

Quentin replaced the sword on its brackets in the wall and carefully closed the glass door over it. He rejoined the Gang just as a White House usher entered the room. He saw Taffy still lying supine, glancing up at him calmly, even forcing a grin. But the usher also saw the wound. Taffy insisted it was not as bad as it looked, a nuisance more than a real injury and, to prove it, he stood up, albeit a little woozily.

The usher would have none of it. He rushed young Taft to the nearby quarters of the First Lady. Quentin and the others followed, several steps behind, ready to recite their fiction as soon as asked. But Edith did not ask. Rather, she took Taffy from the usher and shut the door on the Gang, including her son. She told Taffy to sit and, after examining the wound, which was not, in fact, serious, went to work. Asking a maid for the necessary supplies, she wiped Taffy's face and then cleaned his ear and bandaged it. She was so efficient, she might have been a professional.

But, as the first aid ended, the truth came out, for Edith had interrogated as much as nursed. She dismissed her patient and called in her son. According to one Gang member's report, the scolding he received reached even higher decibel levels than the one to which he was subjected when he lost control of his wagon in a White House corridor and steered himself into a full-length painting of Mrs. Rutherford B. Hayes hanging on a wall. The damage was extensive — some colors smeared, the canvas ripped in a few places. Yet the painting remained in place for many years afterward, the attack on Mrs. Hayes's lower extremities impossible to see. The restoration was little short of a miracle.

"What a *fine* little bad boy he was!" his mother said of Quentin after a few more years had passed. But by then the description had become inadequate to her son's growing complexities.

9

With the Spanish-American war came the emergence of the United States as a world power and the beginning of Theodore Roosevelt as an American power. Suddenly his picture was in all the papers, his opinions were sought on all the issues, and his name was on the lips of everyone who had a thought about current affairs. He would have been the country's most famous celebrity, had the term existed back then, but all was not as glittering as it seemed, at least not initially. Because the Rough Riders were under the jurisdiction of the Army and Roosevelt had still been the Assistant Secretary of the Navy when the group was assembled, he had not been allowed to take a leave of absence to conquer the Spaniards; instead, he was forced to resign. So, once the fighting ended, he found himself — of all things — in need of a job. Theodore Roosevelt was unemployed.

Chauncey Depew, president of the New

York Central Railroad and a few weeks away from being named by the state legislature as the Republican nominee for the U.S. Senate, had something in mind. He wanted Roosevelt to join him on the ticket, to offer himself as a candidate for governor. The governorship already belonged to a Republican, Frank Black, but Black had gotten himself into trouble with his shady financing of the Erie Canal. Some money was missing, unaccounted for — and Black's pockets, according to newspapers and political rivals alike, had suddenly begun to bulge. The connection seemed obvious.

Roosevelt was dubious about running. He had sought the state's top office once before and finished poorly. But that was before the Rough Riders made history under Theodore's baton. Perhaps this time would be different. Depew assured him of it, and so it was. Once he submitted to Depew's entreaties, Theodore campaigned as vigorously as he had once set out to defeat asthma, and with the same results. Roosevelt defeated Black soundly in the Republican gubernatorial primary, and Black won his Senate bid just as easily. In the general election, both Depew and Roosevelt won again, with the latter gaining his office by an even greater margin than he had won the primary. It was beginning to seem that Theodore Roosevelt, as a public figure of one sort or another, could do no wrong.

At the least, he had gotten himself a job.

The Democrats were more than usually upset by the defeat. They were not just opposed to Roosevelt; they were afraid of him. Although the governor of New York has nothing to do with foreign affairs, Roosevelt annoyed his detractors by constantly fulminating on such subjects. In fact, one of his first gubernatorial declarations was to urge a U.S. military invasion of the Philippines. In his view, the natives had begun to behave badly, demanding independence the moment Spain transferred the islands to American rule. This led the *Nation,* already a respected liberal magazine, to refer to the governor's "boyish and unstable mentality." Which, in turn, led Roosevelt to dismiss the *Nation* as a journal of political naïveté.

Worse, though, was the public condemnation Roosevelt suffered from one of his former instructors at Harvard, William James. The nation's leading psychologist, as well as one of its few, James was also a philosopher and a physician, a combination that made him the most respected member of American academe at the time. He brought much of his diverse learning to bear in criticizing his one-time pupil, at whom he had never had a reason to be upset before. Roosevelt, he said, "gushes over war as the ideal condition of human society, for the manly strenuousness which it involves, and treats peace as a condition of blubber-like and swollen ignobility, fit only for huckstering weaklings. . . . To enslave a weak but heroic people, or to brazen out a blunder, is a good enough cause, it appears, for Colonel Roosevelt. To us Massachusetts anti-imperialists, who have fought in better causes, it is not quite good enough. . . . 'Duty and Destiny' have rolled over us like a Juggernaut car."

Although used to shrugging off criticism, Roosevelt was stung by James's vitriol, unable to muster the effort to respond.

Even some members of his own party, though, thought Roosevelt dangerous. High on the list was the man whose position as the most powerful politician in New York State, Thomas "Boss" Platt, was no longer as secure as it had previously been. Platt saw Roosevelt as subversively disobedient: he would not provide sinecures for Platt's henchmen, would not allow state officials to give those henchmen government contracts, and would not excuse them from prison terms if they continued skimming money off the top of those contracts. Frank Black had permitted all of these benefits, in addition to his own skimming. But Roosevelt, following the advice of his spectral mentor, Theodore Senior, would no longer countenance that kind of business as usual.

Platt was furious. This was not how politics was played. Roosevelt's decision to behave ethically meant that the "Boss" no longer had the power to distribute electoral spoils, to reward lackeys; and without that power, was he in reality, not just in name, the head of the party? He quickly determined to get the Rough Rider and his damnable insistence on probity out of New York, and he would do it, he decided, by campaigning for Roosevelt's interment in the tomb of the vice-presidency.

Virtually the entire Republican party came to his aid. Some did so because, like Platt, they despised Roosevelt and wanted him to be virtuous elsewhere. Others did so because, like Roosevelt's dear friend Senator Henry Cabot Lodge, they saw the vice-presidency not as a burial plot but as both a promotion and stepping-stone, and wanted to compensate their man for his heroism in Cuba, eventually, with the highest of national offices.

At first, Roosevelt did not want to be vice president. He believed himself too vital and ambitious a man for what had long been so sedentary a position. But the more he pondered the office, the more he wondered: Did it *have* to be so sedentary? Maybe, just maybe, someone with his ambition and spirit might be able to make something of the office that a lesser man could not. This is how Lodge urged him to think — out of the box, as we would say today. Roosevelt would, after all, have the entire country, even the world, as his domain. As Assistant Secretary of the Navy, he had not behaved as an assistant. As Police Commissioner of New York, he had not behaved as merely a municipal official. And as Governor of New York, he was not allowing himself to be limited by the boundaries of his state. Becoming Vice President of the United States would allow him to more appropriately, and volubly, opine. The position began to seem appealing. Surely the Rooseveltian personality could overcome whatever objections the dour president, William McKinley, might make to a new kind of second-in-command.

After more consideration, and consultation with Lodge and other members of Congress, he made up his mind. Yes, he told his party, delighting both those who loved him and those who reviled him, he would seek the vice-presidency as requested. He would serve as Governor of New York for a single two-year term, then resign to begin the quest for higher office.

In 1900, McKinley was re-elected to the nation's most prestigious office, defeating the eminently defeatable Democrat, William Jennings Bryan, for the second consecutive time. Although wary of Roosevelt's impulsiveness, McKinley had accepted him as his running mate; and both men rejoiced on election night, Roosevelt disingenuously swearing fealty to any and all commands of his superior officer.

No one, though, made merry the way Boss Platt made merry. Yes, Roosevelt was now the second most powerful man in the United States, but only nominally. He would, in truth, have neither the power nor the time to interfere with Platt's New York corruptions. And so the Boss broke out the top-shelf booze, clinked glasses with friends, associates, strangers, hookers — and drank himself into the most blissful haze of his political career.

It would not be long, however, until Platt was reaching for a bottle for different reasons altogether.

10

Meanwhile, to the surprise of no one in the family, Quentin was showing signs of growing into Theodore's son more than Edith's. He exhibited at times an almost "freakish duplication of his father. . . . He had the same . . . clarity of perception, and ability to concentrate totally on any task at hand. Yet, more than any of the other Roosevelt children except Alice — who in any case had a different mother — he had a large personality of his own."

One element of that personality was a bluntness uncommon for his years. Annoyed with one of his nurses for some reason at the age of three and a half, he said to her, "You are the most unpleasant beast I e'er have looked on yet." The poor woman was appalled. Perhaps she would have been less so had she realized that the line was not original. Quentin was, rather, quoting from a ballad that had been read to him recently; he had probably not meant to be so cruel.

Unfortunately, the youngest child duplicated his father in another way as well. Although robust and energetic in his earliest years, he had become sickly as he grew older, plagued by sinus aches, fevers, "the grip," and an operation to remove his adenoids that left him debilitated for much longer than it should have. "Poor Quentin has a severe cough," his mother wrote when he was five, and it was neither the first nor the last with which he was afflicted. At age seven, his father reported, "Quentin's sickness was purely due to a riot in candy and ice cream with chocolate sauce. He was a very sad bunny next morning." Later the same year, he was a sadder bunny. Forced to smoke a cigarette as part of a public-school hazing, he became "sick in the stomach and this completely upset his health so that he is now home and in bed."

He did not like being confined to bed. On another occasion, though, he decided to risk it.

A friend of the family, visiting at Sagamore, come on [Quentin] at Snoulder's drugstore in Oyster Bay, grasping a nickel firmly in his grimy hand and looking longingly at the soda fountain. The friend, knowing that the boy was supposed to be on a diet, remarked: "Quentin, I wouldn't take a soda. It might make you sick."

Quentin looked at the lady with round, solemn eyes. "How sick?" he asked.

"Perhaps sick enough to be sent to bed."

He let her words sink in for a long minute while he weighted profit and loss. Then he deliberately walked forward and deposited his nickel on the counter. "Chocolate sundae, please."

Quentin's most severe disorder struck him a few days after he got a mothball stuck so far up one of his nostrils that he almost swallowed it. All he could say in his defense was that he thought it would fit. It did not. It was, with much embarrassment on the part of the patient, removed by a physician who, while bemused at his task, nonetheless had to perform it with great care. The parents bowed their heads in embarrassment.

Then it hit him — the worst ear infection he had ever had, worse even than the infection brought on a year earlier after another test of body-cavity volume, that time stuffing a pebble into his ear, seeing how far it would go. This latest ailment sent him to the hospital. Coincidentally, his room was directly across the hall from Alice, who was at the same time suffering from an infected jaw.

"[D]octors administered chloroform and lanced his ear," we are told of Quentin's treatment. "For five days doctors asked

Edith to help them hold the child down for syringing treatments which made him 'wake in an agony of apprehension at every footstep or voice' for days afterward. Theodore stayed over at the hospital to help his distressed wife."

Despite her proximity, just a few footsteps away from Quentin's hospital room, Alice did not receive nearly as much attention from her parents as her brother did. Theodore usually looked in on her after he had visited with Quentin but, not having as much to say to a daughter as to a son, spent only a few minutes with her, chatting idly, leaving behind only a few platitudes. Edith, it seems, seldom even entered the room, standing in Alice's doorway and doing little more than smiling and wishing her good luck in her recovery. She was always sincere, but never for more than a few seconds. Alice led the loneliest life of all the Roosevelt siblings, and blamed her stepmother more than anyone else.

Alice had no playmates, for Edith's penchant for privacy extended to her children. Edith didn't step in to fill the gap. She meant to, but she simply couldn't summon the enthusiasm. "I am trying to make Alice more of a companion . . . ," Edith confided to Theodore. "Alice needs someone to laugh and romp with instead of a sober and staid person like me."

How much Edith tried to make Alice more of a companion is open to question. Why Edith did not seek to find her daughter friends of her own age is another question without a known reply. At least in part, the answers to both are probably to be found in Edith's relationship to Alice's late mother, Alice Hathaway Lee. For, ever since she was a child, Edith had believed that she and Teedie would marry — so close was their friendship, so comfortable were they in each other's company. There is, in fact, a photograph believed to date from 1865, thought to show the two of them as six-year-olds, standing in an open window at a Roosevelt apartment on New York's Fifth Avenue and watching the mournful scene below, as Abraham Lincoln's funeral procession passed slowly by.

When the two of them had grown up and Theodore decided instead to marry Alice Lee, Edith was stunned. She should not have been. One of Roosevelt's biographers believes that Miss Lee was "a girl to break a boy's heart." Another writes, "She was, by every surviving account, extraordinarily attractive, slender, graceful in her movements, and 'rather tall' for a girl of that era, five feet seven, which meant that with shoes on she was as tall as [Theodore]. Her hair was a honey-blond and done in fashionable 'water curls' about her temples. . . . She is described repeatedly as 'radiant,' 'bright,' 'cheerful,' 'sunny,' 'high-spirited,' 'enchanting,' 'full of life.' . . ."

As a lady, Edith Carow, who also possessed attributes both physical and otherwise, could not allow herself to show disappointment with Theodore's choice in public. But as a woman, she could not help but feel it to the core. She went to the wedding, an invited guest, a smile chiseled into her face all day, both at the ceremony and at various parties afterward. But her heart had been broken, and when she went home that night, she collapsed from the effort required of her to blend in to the day's festive surroundings. She cried herself to sleep in bewilderment as much as sorrow. And no less in anger, for she felt she was so much the superior of Alice Lee.

Two years after the marriage, when the dreadful dual tragedy struck and Theodore became a youthful widower, Edith started down the path toward becoming Roosevelt's wife after all, his new bride more pleased by her good fortune than she was saddened by the circumstance that had brought it about. She had, of course, not wished Alice Lee ill, and was genuinely upset by her death. But she could not help realizing what Alice Lee's fate would mean to her. How could she think otherwise, after having waited so long and felt so deeply for her man? However, the notion of being a mother in any real sense to Alice Hathaway Lee's daughter was a difficult one, and it is likely that, although Edith might have tried to make young Alice feel like a member of the second Roosevelt family, her resentment for the girl's being the offspring of Theodore's first choice for a wife was simply too strong to be overcome.

As for Theodore, he had his own reasons, already discussed, for distancing himself from his oldest child. She would, thus, never completely outgrow her feeling of being an outsider, a Roosevelt in name only — and, to her regret, that name would change before long.

Taken together, the various illnesses of Quentin's, whatever their cause, made his father uneasy. He could not help but recall his own struggles as a child, and so could not help but fear that Quentin would turn out to be "a little soft," facing even more hardships than his father had. Roosevelt, of course, had cured himself with a Spartan regimen of physical activity. Quentin, his father thought, was not the type to put himself through similar exertion.

But even as an adult, Theodore had his health woes. There was a spell of bronchitis when he was vice president, and a few years later a severe and cursedly enduring leg injury when his presidential carriage collided with a trolley just as it left the White House grounds. A few years after giving up the presidency, he would find himself in South America, struggling mightily to fight off an attack of malaria; and at one point, deciding he could tolerate the disease no more, he resolved to give up the struggle, meet his Maker. If there *was* such a thing as a soft Roosevelt, Theodore could not help but feel at times that *he* was the guilty party, not an offspring.

But these were aberrations, atypical moments in the life of this most durable of men. As for Quentin's ills, however, they were numerous and ongoing. The child would continue to fall victim to various afflictions at various times, but he would surprise his father by subjecting himself to a number of activities to distract himself from discomfort. They would, however, be

89

activities of a different kind from his father's: less vigorous, and more of a trial for others than for himself.

In addition to his ailments, Quentin made his father apprehensive for another reason. As vice president, during visits to Sagamore Hill from Washington, Roosevelt fretted because, on occasion, Quentin performed less than nobly in what might have been the favorite activity of the clan's males. It seems "that Quentin didn't hold his own in the family pillow fights. His tactic was to fall on the pillows and gather them under his arms to prevent his enemies from using them. It was an outrageous ploy to TR, maybe even cowardly." Theodore had more reason to be proud of Ted, Kermit, and Archibald, all of whom threw themselves into the pillow fights with passion, and whose laughter matched their fervor. The older three boys seemed to their father to be the most likely heirs to the tradition of Rooseveltian robustness.

There were a few times, though, when Quentin, rather than being timid, was the aggressor. One day Roosevelt wrote to Kermit, away at Groton, about his and Edith's return from an outing in the country. "When we got home Mother went upstairs first and was met by Archie and Quentin, each loaded with pillows and whispering not to let me know that they were in ambush; then as I marched up to the top they assailed me with shrieks and chuckles of delight and then the pillow fight raged up and down the hall."

Some time afterward, Roosevelt related of his presidential days, he came up the stairs at the White House and discovered Archie "driving Quentin by his suspenders which were fixed to the end of a pair of woolen reins. Then they would ambush me and we would have a vigorous pillow-fight, and after ten minutes of this we would go into Mother's room, and I would read them the book Mother had been reading them. Archie and Quentin are really great playmates."

When the littlest Roosevelt was six, Theodore noted that "Quentin is learning to ride the pony. He had one tumble, which, he remarked philosophically, did not hurt him any more than when I whacked him with a sofa cushion in one of our pillow fights."

Pillow fighting, obviously, though little known to the public, seems to have been as important to the Roosevelts of Sagamore Hill as touch football would later be to the Kennedys of Hyannis Port.

As a youngster, Quentin was often more militant verbally than physically. "Today was Archie's birthday," Roosevelt wrote to Ted, "and Quentin resented Archie's having presents while he (Quentin) had none. With the appalling frankness of three years old, he remarked that 'it made him miserable,' and when taken to task for his lack of altruistic spirit he expressed an obviously perfunctory repentance and said: 'Well, boys must lend boys things, at any rate!' "

His father knew that Quentin was being selfish, but it did not concern him. The boy would outgrow it, no parental lectures necessary. In addition, Theodore secretly admired his son's spunk. The littlest Roosevelt was standing up for himself. As the youngest of six children, it was an indispensable trait.

11

On the last day of August 1901, an anarchist named Leon Czolgosz moved from his family's farm in Warrensville, Ohio, to Buffalo, New York. He took a room in the cheapest hotel he could find and on September 2 bought a gun, a .32-caliber Iver-

Johnson "Safety Automatic." It cost him $4.50, most of what remained to him in the world.

Three days later, Czolgosz stood in a crowd of thousands at the Pan-American Exhibition in Buffalo, where, for a couple of days, President McKinley had been the center of attention. That, Czolgosz thought, was precisely the problem. He was troubled by all the adulation the president received, not only in Buffalo but everywhere else he went: so many people "saluting him, bowing to him, paying homage to him." Czolgosz believed "it wasn't right for one man to get so much ceremony," no matter who he is. It was not his notion of what democracy should be, not a display of all men being equal.

Czolgosz watched McKinley at the Pan-American Exhibition as long as he could, nursing his fury, then went back to his hotel room. That night, alone and with the lock on his door secured, he loaded his weapon and fell into a restless sleep. The next morning, scheduled to be the president's last in Buffalo, Czolgosz awoke early. He splashed cold water on his face and brushed his teeth. Instead of breakfast, he went to a barbershop not only for a haircut, but a shave — a rare treat for himself. Now he

93

was down to his last few pennies. It would hardly matter.

From the barbershop it was back to the hotel to arm himself, then off to the Exhibition to stand in line with a mob of others to meet the president. It took several hours for him to reach the front of the line, but when it was finally Czolgosz's turn to shake the Commander-in-Chief's hand, he instead slapped it away. McKinley looked up, annoyed, puzzled — there was time for no further reaction. Czolgosz pulled the Iver-Johnson out of his pocket, a handkerchief wrapped around his palm, and fired two shots at the president from point-blank range. McKinley staggered forward, with several members of his entourage trying to support him and the rest descending on Czolgosz with fists and curses flying.

"Go easy on him, boys," McKinley is supposed to have said, in a voice so weak as to be barely audible. Then he passed out. It took more than a week for him to die.

Roosevelt was immediately summoned to the presidential bedside. He spent a few days there; then, when McKinley surprised his doctors by improving slightly, he was told he could leave. His departure, reasoned Mark Hanna, McKinley's campaign manager and top adviser, would reassure the nation that the president was on his way to recovery. It would also reassure Hanna, who did not care for Roosevelt any more than Boss Platt had, and had in fact pleaded with Republicans not to nominate him for the second most powerful office in the country. He's a "wildman," Hanna screeched when learning that his advice had been ignored. "Don't any of you realize that there's only one life between this madman and the Presidency!"

Roosevelt, who was just as pleased to bid farewell to Hanna as Hanna was to say his own good-byes, departed immediately and rejoined his family at a camp in the Adirondacks where they had been vacationing. He swam with his children and went exploring with them, hiked with them and chased them through the woods, helped them gather the wood for the fire and cook the meals. At night, Roosevelt told his usual tales to the younger ones, perhaps running out of fuel for repetitions of Kettle Hill by this time, and, with his wife by his side, tucked everybody in with words of love and comfort. The fire crackled as the family drifted off to sleep.

The camp was a remote one. So remote, in fact, that when McKinley finally lost his life, it took twelve hours for a messenger from Buffalo to reach the new president and notify him to report for duty. During those twelve hours, the United States officially had no chief executive.

Roosevelt was numb. As far as he knew, McKinley had been improving; he had not even been thinking about his boss's health. Edith and the children were no less taken aback: shocked by McKinley's death, unable to imagine what it meant for themselves, but certain that their lives would evermore be different.

As Theodore dashed back to the site of the Pan-American Exhibition, his family packed up the camp and returned to Sagamore Hill to start more packing for their new lives. And, in Quentin's case, to pay his respects to the old. Closing in on four now and able to understand something of the world around him, he asked for a piece of black fabric and cut it into small strips. Next he collected all the dolls in his nursery and stood them in a line. He made armbands out of the dark cloth and slipped one on each of his figures. He saluted. "For President McKinley," he explained sadly, then went outside to play with Ted in the sandbox.

His father would not be equally sensitive.

■ ■ ■ ■

Roosevelt had remained out of the public eye during the eight days when McKinley fought for his life. On the ninth, he could hide no longer. Nor did he want to. He was hurriedly inaugurated in the parlor of a private home in Buffalo, becoming from coast to coast and around the world the center of attention, precisely the location he liked best. Or, as his daughter Alice put it, "father wants to be the bride at every wedding and the corpse at any funeral." He was now more visible than either.

Lincoln Steffens, as perceptive as any journalist of the time, was watching as the new Commander-in-Chief began a series of meetings with the public, the press, and members of the McKinley administration, who were his inheritance. The purpose of the sessions was to inform the country and those who helped govern it that all would proceed as the previous president had intended before he was slain. But Steffens was dubious. He did not think Roosevelt's agenda was the same as McKinley's, and, by claiming it was, he had not been telling the truth; Roosevelt was placating the nation rather than informing it, which, Steffens had to concede, might have been, at a time like this, the definition of good politics.

But as he later wrote, Steffens did not like what he saw in the early stages of Roosevelt's tenure. He "strode triumphant among us, talking and shaking hands, dictating and signing letters, and laughing," Steffens observed. "Washington, the whole country was in mourning, and no doubt the President thought he should hold himself down; he didn't; he tried to, but his joy showed in every word and movement. I think he thought he was suppressing his feelings."

A few days after Steffens recorded these impressions, he and Roosevelt took a walk around the White House grounds, accompanied by another journalist, William Allen White, author and editor of the Emporia, Kansas *Gazette,* but much more nationally known and respected than such a position would suggest. It was a brisk walk, the strides long and bold, Roosevelt unable to contain his enthusiasm. Steffens provided details. "With his feet, his fists, his face and with free words [Roosevelt] laughed at his luck. He laughed at the rage of Boss Platt and the tragic disappointment of Mark Hanna; these two had not only lost their

President McKinley but had been given as a substitute the man they thought they had entombed in the vice-presidency. T.R. yelped at their downfall. And he laughed with glee at the power and place that had come to him."

Steffens did not dislike the new president; in fact, he was engaged by him, finding him a fascinating character, a man of great and broadly based intelligence and little regard for politics as usual. But he was offended by the callousness with which Theodore, at least in private, had assumed his new office, and thus could not make up his mind about the new resident of the White House. In print, however, he kept his reservation to himself.

12

The Roosevelts were an epistolary clan. A large, boisterous family, each member seemed curious about the other, and some of them stayed in touch with their fellow Roosevelts virtually every day of their lives: parents with children, siblings with siblings, in-laws with in-laws, nieces and nephews with aunts and uncles, relatives twice-removed with other relatives thrice-removed. They would write about major events, such as how Theodore had fared in

Cuba and how he was about to fare as president, but they could also fill paragraphs, and sometimes pages, with gossip, speculation, the smallest of details of life around them: for instance, an observation about the daughters of casual friends who "have grown to be big . . . girls with very short skirts." Meaning, in all likelihood, that their ankles showed.

When Roosevelt succeeded McKinley, he was separated from those he loved more than ever before. There were presidential trips to Yale for its bicentennial, to Harvard and Stanford and other universities for speeches, and to New York for a variety of occasions. Theodore went to Memphis to address the Deep Waterways Convention and to Panama to check on construction of the canal. He traveled to the Minnesota State Fair to glad-hand, to New England for a series of partisan political speeches, to Sharon Springs, Kansas, for religious services, and to the West and Deep South for annual hunting trips, about which more will be revealed later.

Meanwhile, Edith and the children made trips of their own, leaving Washington every June to spend the summers at Sagamore Hill, which now had its own telephone so that Roosevelt could easily be reached on those occasions when he got away from the White House to enjoy a long weekend with the family. But the phone was for government use only, not personal conversations among the family.

Letters became more important to the Roosevelts than ever.

And, in some ways, they became most important to Quentin. Before he had anything substantial to say, barely before he could hold a pencil, he was writing postcards to Washington. In what is believed to be the first that survives, he says:

Dear Father,
  Please bring me a mountain . . .

Probably a few months later:

Dear Father,
  It has snowed here. Goodby.
                                  Kisses, Quentin

Later still, the child's grip on the pencil more firm now and his artistic skills having reached the point at which he could draw a rather smug-looking swine out for a stroll:

This pig is sent to you dear Father from Quentin.

In what seems to have been the longest of his early missives, Roosevelt's youngest son even chastised him for failing to write more to his wife. In block letters:

DEAR FATHER,
  I HOPE YOU ARE WELL . . . ALL MOTHERS LETTERS WERE LATE FROM YOU.
    YOUR LOVING, QUENTIN ROOSEVELT

Theodore responded to his children's messages quickly and eagerly. He wrote to "Blessed Ted." He wrote to "Darling Kermit." And he wrote to "Dear Quenty-quee." On White House stationery, upon which he had drawn a bunny and a turtle, he told Quentin, then seven and at Sagamore Hill, what he had recently witnessed in Washington:

The other day when out riding what should I see in the road ahead of me but a real B'rer Terrapin and B'rer Rabbit. They were sitting solemnly beside one another and looked just as if they had come out of a book; but as my horse walked along B'rer Rabbit went hippity hippity hippity off into the bushes and B'rer Terrapin drew in his head and legs

till I passed.
Your loving father, Theodore Roosevelt.

A few days earlier the president had drawn a zookeeper feeding an elk on his White House paper. But he began by describing something other than his visit to the Washington Zoo:

Blessed Quenty-quee,
The little birds in the nest in the vines on the garden fence are nearly grown up. Their mother still feeds them.

And there followed yet another drawing, Momma bird hovering over her young with a worm in her mouth.
Two years after that, Roosevelt wrote a poem for Quentin as if Quentin himself had been the author:

When I went to sleep at night
In my little bed
I dreamed I saw a goblin
Standing near my head. . . .

At the time, the verse seemed but a trifle. It wasn't. Neither Quentin nor his father had any idea how prescient the notion of a goblin, or some such creature of the night, would turn out to be.

Quentin wrote to other Roosevelts too. One summer, when his mother was at the White House for a few weeks with his father, leaving the children in charge of their nannies and servants, her impatient littlest boy made a request of her.

what day do you come back will you get me a game of going to the north pole. I will send you the ten cents for it. . . .

And he communicated with his mother's sister, his aunt "emely," even before he had learned to spell her name correctly:

I am having a Butterfly collection in oyster bay and invermont [environ-ment]. We saw twelve monerk [monarch] buterflys in our Garden in oyster bay.

Later in the same note:

I have been feeling quite well except for almost every night I would have a pain from eating [White House physician and Admiral] Doctor Rixey's chestnuts they were so good.

No one in the family wrote more letters

than Quentin during his Sagamore Hill summers. He wanted to be like everyone else. He wanted everyone else to include him. Which they did, so that, as far back as he could remember, he would always think of himself as an important member of the tribe. And he always was.

13

In the autumn, winter, and spring, Quentin lived mostly in the White House, and the White House was no place to raise someone like Quentin Roosevelt. Not with its elegant furnishings, its rich historical ambience, and the central position it occupied in national and international affairs. Not with so many diplomats and politicians coming and going, with White House police and fleets of security guards ever on duty. One would not invite Tarzan to a tea party; neither should one have housed young Quentin for nine months a year at the nation's most prestigious address. Nor should his father have been so accepting of the child's rowdiness.

In fact, there were times when Theodore actually partook of the rowdiness; he was, in the words of biographer Edmund Morris, "capable of considerable mischief himself." In honor of such behavior, the White

House Gang bestowed a singular honor upon the president of the United States. It designated him an honorary member of the Gang, and since a friend would later describe Roosevelt as a perpetual six-year-old, he easily met the age requirement. He was known, for instance, to engage in childish contortions of the visage, sometimes on inappropriate occasions. "One of these appeared on the spring afternoon when Roosevelt departed from the White House in his carriage. As he reached the front gate, he leaned out the window, looked behind him, and made 'grotesque faces.' A crowd had gathered at the front gate of the mansion, hoping for a glimpse of the chief executive — and when they got it they were astonished. They got to see the President of the United States, all right, but he was twisting up his face as if having a fit of some kind!"

What they did not know was that Theodore was continuing his child's play with Quentin, who was himself making grotesque faces as he stood in the doorway behind the carriage. Father and son grimaced at each other, growled at each other, each trying to make the other break out in laughter.

Family friend and later Roosevelt biographer Hermann Hagedorn wrote of another incident of distorted faces involving the president and the White House Gang.

There was the occasion when the boys were riding on the back seat of a trolley-car making faces at everybody who went by in carriages, and especially the bearded dignitaries. Up from the White House came the President's open carriage, with the President in the rear seat. The boys made their worst faces, and the President responded with grimaces of his own. As the car halted in a tangle of traffic and the presidential carriage stood for a moment next the rear of the car, the President leaned forward and, in a voice clearly audible to everyone in the car, said "Quentin Roosevelt and you other little rascals, I think you have very nearly succeeded in making a fool of me in public. I had the idea of asking you to hop in, and ride the rest of the way with me. On second thought I have concluded that it is entirely too dangerous for me to be seen with you."

The colored coachman and footman lost their decorum and grinned as the carriage swept forward and away.

It was a priceless relationship.

From his White House office one day, Roosevelt called the War Department and told a dispatcher to send a message to the Gang ordering them to cease their "attack on this building" without further delay. Quentin received the warning, on official War Department letterhead, and read it aloud. The boys, abashed, looked at each other timidly, quizzically, wondering what they had done to deserve such a warning. What kind of trouble were they in now?

None, concluded the ever-suspicious and frequently perceptive Quentin, after taking some time to think things through. He knew his father's sense of humor, and this was it. There was only a president of the United States behind the threat, he told his accomplices in deviltry, not the War Department. He tossed the letter away, and the Gang went on to plan its next escapade.

Like his father, Quentin was both untrained and charming, a combination that, in the boy's case, was best beheld at a distance, especially when he was in possession of his trusty bow and arrow. So frequent, in fact, was his use of the weapon that there is a portrait of the youngster as archer on a second-floor wall at Sagamore Hill. His hair is gold. He is wearing a white shirt, a white skirt, and an expression so beatific that he looks for all the world like the embodiment of Edenic innocence.

There is no portrait of an unsuspecting target being struck with the weapon.

As far as anyone knows, Quentin never fired at law enforcement officials. However, he attacked them in other ways, having apparently decided that the more authoritative the figure, the more suitable he was as a victim. For instance, a White House policeman. Quentin from the roof of the national manse had "been known to drop projectiles, including a snowball so gigantic it completely flattened one officer, to the uncontrollable hilarity of the President. . . ." He had also been known to gather other members of the White House Gang and follow the Executive Mansion's lamplighter around the grounds at night. "After he lighted a lamp," writes family historian Allen Churchill, "one of the boys climbed up the pole and blew it out."

Roosevelt also had a difficult time controlling his hilarity when Quentin interrupted a meeting between his father and Attorney General Philander Knox. The two men heard the boy enter the room, looked up, and saw him standing with a four-foot king snake coiled around him. And, as if one reptile weren't enough, in each of his hands was a smaller snake, writhing for solid ground. The attorney general's eyes widened to twice their normal aperture and he slid back his chair. The president took the sight in stride.

"As Quentin and his menagerie were an interruption to my interview with the Department of Justice," Roosevelt would write of the incident, "I suggested that he go into the next room, where four Congressmen were drearily waiting until I should be at leisure. I thought that he and his snakes would probably enliven their waiting time. He at once fell in with the suggestion and rushed up to the Congressmen with the assurance that he would there find kindred spirits. They at first thought the snakes were wooden ones, and there was some perceptible recoil up when they realized that they were alive. Then the king snake went up Quentin's sleeve . . . and we hesitated to drag him back because his scales rendered that difficult. The last I saw of Quentin, one Congressman was gingerly helping him off with his jacket, so as to let the snake crawl out of the upper end of his sleeve."

The next day, the incident was reported in the *New York Times*.

Quentin often accompanied his practical jokes with a subtler form of humor, a wit that revealed intellectual precocity rare for his years, whatever they happened to be. At age ten, for instance, on a day when his legs were stinging from a terrible sunburn, he looked down at them and said to his father, "They look like a Turner sunset, don't they?"

Then he paused, glanced up, and firmly resolved, "I won't be caught again this way! quoth the raven, 'Nevermore.' "

Theodore smiled at him, squeezing his shoulder, and, for as long as the president could spare from his official duties, the two of them went on to discuss matters other than charred legs and affairs of state.

On another occasion, Quentin managed to attach a stamp to the neck of his friend, young master Looker, without Looker's knowing it. Then, even more deftly, with Looker again remaining oblivious, he wrote across the back of his Eton collar: "If not delivered, return to White House, Wash., D.C." It seems unlikely that Looker did not feel Quentin's writing implement; but in his book about the Gang, Looker swears the incident actually happened.

Quentin did not, however, usually operate solo in his prank-pulling, mirth-making, or hell-raising. As the leader of the White House Gang, whose headquarters were the building's attic, he usually had several minions standing by waiting for orders, Looker being one of them. Together, they collaborated on such adventures as firing water pistols at one another in the East Room, racing bicycles through the east corridor, shooting arrows at a cat tethered to a rock by a clothesline, and hurling spitballs both at teachers in school and paintings on the White House walls, especially one of Andrew Jackson, to which so many little orbs were salivarily attached, Looker claimed, "that we dragged a chair under the portrait to arrange the wet lumps in designs — three on his forehead, 'like an Arabian dancer,' Quentin said, and one on the lobe of either ear. A poultice of masticated newspaper was set upon the end of his nose 'to scare the flies away,' and a gob over each of the buttons on his coat."

Not all of these pranks pleased the president. When he saw the expectoration-loaded gobs of paper on Jackson and other figures adorning his residence, Roosevelt "pulled Quentin out of bed and had him take them all off the portraits, and this morning required him to bring in the three other culprits before me. I explained to them that they had acted like boors, that it would have been a disgrace to have behaved so in any gentleman's house, but that it was a double disgrace in the house of the Nation. . . . They were four very sheepish small boys when I got through with them!" the president crowed. Especially sheepish was Quentin, who was banned from membership in the Gang until his father thought enough time had passed to constitute suitable punishment.

The Gang was also humbled after Roosevelt saw them tormenting the tethered cat. "If you capture something really *sporting* to shoot at — something fast, and strong, and dangerous to life and limb — please let me know at once. Otherwise, I shall not be interested, nor, do I think, should you."

In other words, there were rules for play as unyielding as those for work. A person should choose as an opponent only one who had a fighting chance. An attack upon a harmless feline who had been denied the freedom to run for safety was beneath the dignity of the kind of man Roosevelt wanted his son to be.

Actually, Quentin and associates received a number of presidential reprimands, one of which brought a reprimand from Quentin in return. When he took it upon himself one day to walk through a White House garden on stilts, mashing flowers as he teetered his

113

way along, the president left his office, ran downstairs, and snapped at him. Whereupon his son, having grown tired of such responses, replied, "I don't see what good it does me for you to be president. I can't do anything here. I wish I was back home."

Roosevelt's response is not known.

The occasion for one of the president's most severe tongue-lashings was a civil war of sorts among members of the Gang. It seems that the boys had split into two factions and engaged in what is known to history — a very minor sub-section of history — as the Battle of Guidon. Quentin Roosevelt headed one side, Charles "Taffy" Taft the other.

At issue was a "moth-eaten silk artillery pennant," the guidon. As the conflict began, it was in the possession of Company Q (Quentin). It was desired, however, by Company T (Taffy). The two sides engaged in conflict over it, with the understanding that whichever team could maintain possession of the pennant for three consecutive minutes "would win the privilege of dictating Gang activities for the rest of the afternoon."

As should be apparent by this time, Earle Looker had as an adult appointed himself the Gang's unofficial historian. Here is how he remembers the hostilities:

During the ensuing battle, Taffy, by far the largest combatant, maintained his grasp of the flagstaff and ordered an aide, Edward "Slats" Stead, to spin a concealed tap. Q and his force of three men were blasted head over heels in the resultant gush of water. Enraged, Q issued a counterorder ("Keep it up! Keep it up! I'm going to sinister this, immejitly!") and disappeared. Suddenly, the gush lost its force. As the spray cleared, Q was revealed in possession of a fire ax, with which he had sliced the hose into several sections. His triumph was forestalled by a stentorian shout from the West Wing, and the President came charging through the Rose Garden, coattails flying.

Roosevelt was irate. Edmund Morris has published the dialogue between father and son.

TR . . . When the action is wrong, you must admit it, and correct it by some further action —

Q (looking at the severed hose) I don't see

how this can be corrected.

TR Only by an entirely new garden-hose. It was Government property. . . . It will cost money, part of that which I am earning — or was earning, when interrupted by a dispatch regarding the progress of this war, and left hurriedly for the field.

Q Well, of course, you're right; but we've learned our lesson, you know —

TR We? Don't you mean yourself? And what have you learned?

Q Not to cut up garden hoses.

TR And not to use fire-axes on anything but a fire —

Q *(with a touch of wistfulness)* We're not so likely to have a fire.

TR Not with all this water around! You escape, Quentin, only because of the extenuating circumstances, arising out of the heat of battle .

Quentin's relief was visible. His father knew from personal experience what it was like in the heat of *real* battle, that a fellow

116

could suffer a lapse in judgment, and therefore he would not berate his son for so understandable an offense.

And with that, we are told, the president "turned on his heel and marched back to the executive office." His boy returned to his mates, both friend and foe, and declared that the Battle of Guidon had come to an inglorious end. There was no victor.

"Swollen noses, split lips and black eyes were freely given and taken by Quentin," wrote Looker. But it may be that the prank he found most satisfying was also a favor for a loved one. For instance, Quentin would long recall the spring afternoon on which Archie was ill and confined to bed. He could look out his White House window at a clear, sunny day, perfect for galloping through the parks of the nation's capital on his pony, but he could not take advantage of it. He was as gloomy as a Washington sky in winter.

Quentin, large-hearted by nature, could not help but feel his brother's disappointment. Then he got an idea. It was risky, physically demanding, but. . . .

With the help of a White House footman, the boy wedged Archie's steed Algonquin, all 350 pounds of him, into a freight elevator — Quentin pulling the reins, the doorman shouldering the animal's rear flanks. The doors closed behind Algonquin, his tail barely making it in, and he neighed frightfully at the close quarters. Then he "became interested in his own reflection in the elevator mirror, enabling the footman to press the second floor button." The elevator chugged and squealed slowly to the second floor.

Whereupon the doors opened and the pony trotted uncertainly into the corridor, still needing the occasional push from behind. Quentin and the footman steered him to Archie's room, hopeful that the mere sight of him would raise the patient's spirits. And it did, which in turn raised Quentin's spirits, considering all the trouble through which he had gone. Also raised were Algonquin's spirits, as Archie sat up in bed and stroked him, talking to him and feeding him from the bag of oats Quentin had thoughtfully brought along — with the patient, all the while, not feeling nearly so indisposed as before. It was perfect, thought Quentin: a violation of decorum that had no victim, only a beneficiary.

Well, it was perfect for a few minutes. After which, unfortunately, Algonquin's spirits soared a little *too* high, and his whinnies of delight gave him away. The White House gendarmes arrived and, finding an equine in an executive mansion bedroom, promptly marched him out. Since he's already here, Quentin would likely have reasoned, why not let him stay? You can only take him away once anyhow. But it was too much logic for an adult mind. The young horse was stuffed into the elevator again and returned to his stable, thereby ruining the rest of the day for boys and beast alike.

As might be expected, with only three years separating them, Quentin and Archie had a special affinity for each other; Quentin would, in fact, serve as best man at Archie's wedding-in-a-hurry before the Great War. Their father also had a special affinity for his two youngest. In writing to Ted, who was away at Groton and had never had a relapse of his headaches and "nervous prostration," Roosevelt said: "Recently I have gone in to play with Archie and Quentin after they have gone to bed, and they have grown to expect me, jumping up, very soft and warm in their tummies, expecting me to roll them over on the bed."

When Archie and Quentin were ready for the classroom, they went to a public school named Force, which was close to the White

House but of no particular distinction.

Quentin showed promise in his first year: an "excellent" every month in Grammar and Language; all "excellents" and one "good" in Arithmetic; and four "excellents" and three "goods" in Reading. His first Penmanship grade was an "F" for "fair," but by the end of the second semester he had achieved excellence here as well.

Archie's grades were also above average, but like his brother he took his studies casually, the two of them relying instead on natural intelligence and their foundation of home learning rather than diligent application to their lessons.

Sometimes Quentin and Archie walked to school. On other occasions they roller-skated or rode their ponies. They might arrive on time, they might arrive ten or fifteen minutes late. It did not matter to them. It did, of course, matter to their teachers, and it happened often enough that tension began to build, tension of which the boys were oblivious.

On the way home, Theodore's sons would also take their time, in no hurry to begin their nightly assignments. They would look into shop windows, buy themselves an ice cream, and often pay a visit to the local firehouse, where the men on duty allowed them to slide down the pole until their hands were raw and the insides of their knees sore.

During the boys' first year at Force, the president received a visitor from Europe who told him how surprised she was that he allowed his children to "sit side by side with the children of working men in a public school." Roosevelt stifled his impulse to respond angrily. Democracy, he said in effect, was not just a form of government for Americans, but a way of life. His family, he told her, was among the many that practiced it.

Shortly afterward, Roosevelt told his friend the Western novelist Owen Wister of a similar encounter, this one involving Quentin and a haughty matron he encountered at a White House social function. She, too, knew that the youngest two Roosevelt children attended Force and wondered why.

"How do you get along with those common boys?" the woman wanted to know.

Quentin looked away for a moment before answering. "I don't know what you mean," he told her. "My father says there are only four kinds of boys: good boys and bad boys and tall boys and short boys; that's all the kinds of boys there are."

Roosevelt, he said to Wister, was "dee-lighted" with Quentin's response.

When Edith heard of Quentin's response, she was as proud as her husband had been.

But where Quentin was concerned, the good seemed always to come with the bad. Or, less harshly, the cherubic with the disruptive. His academic performances were inconsistent; although usually outstanding, he could sometimes take nosedives into mediocrity — depending on the subject, his mood on a given day, the current schemes of the White House Gang and the amount of time they required, and the demands of other extracurricular, sometimes spur-of-the moment, activities.

And all too frequently it was impossible to tell *how* Quentin was doing; he would hand in papers so messy that they could not be read, either because of hurriedly sloppy handwriting, smeared ink, or dirt stains. It was these breaches of conduct that led a teacher at Force, Miss Virginia Arnold, to write to the nation's most powerful man, complaining that his son "is wasting his time in school in play. . . .

"Today at ten minutes past nine he entered school, singing, flourishing his hands and in general disorder, which continued after he had taken his seat. This disorder and spirit of play was not only consuming his time but was disturbing the entire class which was earnestly working until he entered. . . ."

Miss Arnold thought that, as the boy's father, the President of the United States should pay a visit to the school office. Roosevelt replied promptly.

Dear Miss Arnold:

I thank you for your note about Quentin. Don't you think it would be well to subject him to stricter discipline — that is, punish him yourself, or send him to Mr. Murch [the principal]? Mrs. Roosevelt and I have no scruples whatever against corporal punishment. . . .

I do not think I ought to be called in merely for such offenses as dancing when coming into the classroom, for singing higher than the other boys, or for failure to work as he should at his examples, or for drawing pictures instead of doing his sums.

My own belief is that he is a docile child, although one that needs a firmness that borders on severity. If you find him defying your authority or committing any serious misdeeds let me know and I will whip him. . . .

He found Miss Arnold's letter bothersome, and his response showed it, although in restrained fashion. But it seems fair to say that, in reality, he was taking out his frustrations on the teacher, and the source of those frustrations was his son. Theodore was busy enough running a country; he did not need to increase his workload by issuing reprimands to Quentin for behavior so ill-mannered that there could be no excuse for it. His son was smarter than that. He was too courteous to disrupt a classroom, too respectful. Roosevelt did not understand. There was no reason for the actions of which his son was so often guilty. As a result, it did not take long for the president to make good on the threat contained in the last paragraph of the missive above. "Quentin has left school without permission," he wrote, "and told untruths about it; I have to give him a severe whipping. Mother and I are worried about him."

Perhaps it was a phase, they thought, something age-related; he would outgrow it. His older brothers, though, had never strolled into class late, "singing, flourishing [their] hands and in general disorder . . . disturbing the entire class. . . ." It seemed, then, to be Quentin's phase alone.

■ ■ ■ ■

The letter from Miss Arnold, and Roosevelt's responses, both verbal and physical, were not brought to the public's attention. They did not fit the image the journalists had begun to construct for Quentin. The boy's rebuke to the "haughty society matron," however, was a story reported by newspapers all over the nation, as were his pony delivery to Archie and some of the White House Gang's tamer breaches of etiquette, such as the water-pistol warfare in the executive mansion. It is no wonder, then, that the last-born of the Roosevelts "became the country's little boy," a source of innocent amusement to all who read about him, as if he were one of those charming scamps in the funny pages of the New York tabloids, which were becoming all the rage during the Roosevelt presidency. Thus the journalistic search for a real-life version of Little Sammie Sneeze of the *Herald,* Little Jimmy of the *Journal,* and Foxy Grandpa's grandchildren in the *American.* The president's son, at least as portrayed in the press, made of the trio an ideal quartet. He was "adored not just for his democratic spirit but for such things as bringing a piglet home by streetcar and inviting his class-mates to play baseball on the White House lawn."

The little pig amused the president. The diamond carved into a portion of the White House lawn did not, even though, his father later crowed, "Quentin is really beginning to know a little about baseball," and further bragged that a team of which he was captain "has been christened the Invincibles, be-cause of the number of its victories!"

And so the president's often-contradictory reactions to his Quenty-quee: he approved and chastised, laughed and fumed, nodded his head and shook his fist. It is not unusual. A child who is his father's favorite stirs strong emotions; he is, thus, more likely to become the father's *bête noire* now and then than one of the other children, and although Quentin did not often feel the sting of his father's disapproval, he felt it deeply when it came.

Perhaps this is why, when a reporter asked Quentin what the daily routine was like for the president at the White House, he replied, "I see him occasionally, but I know nothing of his family life." He was kidding, of course, displaying the same droll sense of humor that led him to compare his sun-scorched legs to a Turner sunset. But it is interesting that he chose to kid in such a manner.

The adored parent, in all likelihood, becomes a *bête noire* to the child at times, too.

At his worst, though, Quentin was not nearly the headache for the president that his oldest daughter was. For the most part, Roosevelt himself deserved the blame, never giving Alice the attention he gave his other children, usually including her in family functions but seldom in the camaraderie that grew out of them. Except on the rarest occasions, he did not mention her in his correspondence, and when he talked to her there was seldom warmth in his voice, sometimes not even eye contact.

There were also examples, although not many, of what can only be interpreted as deliberate cruelty. "Although I like swimming," Alice wrote, long after the incident, "I couldn't dive. I can see my father at Sagamore shouting to me from the water, 'Dive, Alicy, dive.' And there I was trembling on the bank saying through tears, 'Yes, Father,' to this sea monster who was flailing away in the water, peering near-sightedly at me without glasses and with his mustache glistening in the sunlight. It was pathetic."

And the hostility that grew out of the incident stayed with her for years. "I cried, I snarled, I hated."

But Theodore and Edith were not alone in alienating Alice. Quentin was sometimes part of the problem too. He would taunt Alice in childishly unmerciful ways, although probably because she was his elder, not his step-sister. Which is to say that his antics were the natural unruliness of little boys, not the result of an insidious brand of family politics.

At one point, Alice said, Quentin had "a trick of whenever he sees me, of putting his thumb in his mouth and then taking it out and offering it to me to suck!" Alice would fume, and sometimes chase her tormentor through the corridors at Sagamore. Quentin would dash for refuge in an upstairs storage room upon which, hoping to dissuade his sister from further pursuit, he had painted the words — or, in his case, word — DOOR-LOCKED.

By the time an undeterred Alice also burst through the door of the storage room, Quentin had climbed out the window onto the roof of the porch. From there he could slide down the drainpipe to the ground, where Archie, who knew what was happening, might be waiting. The two of them would run across the lawn into the woods, laughing at big sis, who was not enough of a tomboy to give pursuit. She would yell at her stepbrothers until they were too deep in the woods to hear her anymore.

Theodore, even when he knew of such incidents, does not seem to have been angry at the perpetrators.

When Alice was seventeen, Edith decreed that she would have no official duties at White House functions. The girl, not surprised by her exclusion, had already plotted her revenge. No official duties? All right, then there would be a number of *un*official duties, self-chosen, all for the purpose of revenge. She took to "smoking, drinking, racing a car, betting on the horses," and complaining to pencil-ready reporters that punch had been served at one of the White House galas instead of champagne.

And it got worse. "Princess Alice," as she was soon known in the public prints, "became a regular in the most virulent of gossip sheets, *Town Topics.* Edith was horrified."

It was believed, in fact, that Alice's decision to marry Ohio Congressman Nicholas Longworth, fourteen years her senior, bald as a croquet ball, paunchy, his intelligence of limited scope even by general legislative standards — and perhaps even less attractive in person than he sounds — had more to do with getting away from her parents than it did with Longworth's charms.

Those charms, however, sometimes proved to be considerable. A well-known ladies' man before his marriage, he became an adulterer afterward, inspiring his wife to engage in a long-running affair of her own.

It was all a source of great humiliation to Theodore and Edith. Alice, in many ways a tortured young woman, took great satisfaction in being the cause.

Her behavior notwithstanding, Theodore insisted that "I love all these children." Continuing, he told a reporter that he had "great fun with them and am touched by the way in which they feel that I am their special friend, champion, and companion." In addition to being pillow fighters, they were hide-and-seekers, snipers and gigglers, teasers and practical jokers, and often even wrestlers. Theodore was always "It" in games of tag and often played scary bear with his youngsters, chasing them through the house, even the White House, while comically growling at them; and when he caught them, picking them up and turning them upside down and whirling them around. He would growl menacingly. They would shriek in pleasure. Often, Quentin and some of the Gang members played "chase the president . . . in the murky attic of the White House," where the shrieks echoed when they caught Theodore. At Sagamore, in the mornings, he would lead them on horseback over the same trails he had ridden as a child.

And then, all of a sudden, he would settle the children, insist on their silence, and further insist that they grasp the beauty as their father recited poetry to them, poetry he had memorized in his bedridden days as an asthmatic child. Their budding lives could not consist entirely of games, he believed; they must be full, must have breadth.

But Roosevelt knew each of his children was different from the others, and treated them accordingly. Ted was a budding military man, and he and his father often talked about both the history and strategy of warfare, with Ted firing questions and his father shooting back the responses. Writing to him from the White House when he was sixteen, he wondered "if you are old enough yet to care for a good history of the American Revolution. If so, I think I shall give you mine by Sir George Trevelyan; although

131

it is by an Englishman, I really think it on the whole the best account I have ever read. If I give it to you, you must be very careful of it, because he sent it to me himself." Young Ted could not have been more pleased. He handled the volume as if it were made of precious metal, reading it diligently and returning it to his father in precisely the same condition in which it had been given to him. He would one day become, he believed, a more capable soldier for his exposure to Trevelyan.

As for the younger children, according to H. W. Brands, Kermit had begun growing into "a solemn, cunning mite . . . [with] a really deep little nature under it all."

Ethel still possessed the leadership qualities she had always shown, even as a three-year-old, when she was a "bustling person, [and] a born manager who orders [her brothers] about constantly." The day would come, although not for many years, when she would order her father about, earning his displeasure as she helped to save his life.

As for the youngest two imps, Archie was a "merry, pretty mischief," just the sort to appeal to Theodore's six-year-old side, as was Quentin, whose father was pleased to note was becoming "more cunning every day."

Theodore Roosevelt almost certainly combined the presidency with parenthood better than any other man in American history, devoting more time and care to his children, and taking more pleasure in their company, than any of our nation's other chief executives — and this despite his official duties, which he never neglected. But neither did he neglect his children, who were always on his mind, if not always in his presence. It was as if he had figured out a way to live days that were more than twenty-four hours.

There were times, however, when Edith had to pull in the reins on her husband, telling him there was entirely too much "tickle and grabble" going on, and that henceforth he was to partake of such games with Archie and Quentin before dinner and only then. Abashed and unhappy, the three of them agreed. As the most mature member of the family, Edith had the final word on frolicking.

Theodore was a roughhouser with all of his boys. But although he had plenty of affection to go around, and thus did not seem to cause any jealousies among his herd of offspring, he clearly showed more affection to Quentin than to any of the others. One afternoon early in the Roosevelt presidency, when the family was driving up Pennsylvania Avenue, heading for the Washington Naval Yard and a few days of relaxation on the *Sylph,* it was Quentin whom the president publicly embraced. Afterward he kissed him, "first on one chubby cheek, then on the other."

A year later, when older brother Ted was away at boarding school, his father confided in him about his youngest sibling. "Until Quentin goes to bed the house is entirely lively," Roosevelt said. "After that the rooms seem big and lonely and full of echoes."

It could have been an indelicate thing to say if Ted had been the jealous sort. He could have assumed that his father had never said anything like that about him, and felt a sharp jolt of resentment. But Ted's thoughts did not run in that direction. More likely, he was pleased that Theodore had taken him into his confidence as he had — just two adults talking about adulthood's issues. Which is to say, the president was, in effect, complimenting Ted by recognizing that his oldest son was mature enough to realize that, with his siblings gone or soon to be departing, his father was entitled to feel emptiness encroaching. Roosevelt's comment to Ted simply acknowledged that the youngest and most spirited of his children was bound to take on extra importance as the others pursued their educations. And besides, Ted and his father had their own private relationship based on the study of military matters.

Less obviously, Quentin was also Edith's favorite, "the cleverest" of her children. She might have had an extra affection for him as well because, although she would never admit such a thing to her husband, there were already signs that Quentin was the "least martial" of the children. What she tolerated in her husband she did not want to encourage in her young ones.

14

The White House years were the most remarkable in Roosevelt's remarkable public life. They were, in fact, something of a miracle — and not just because of the time he found for his children while guiding his country to world prominence. It is because of the time he *didn't* find for hostilities with other nations, among other reasons, that his presidency stands out in such bold relief. One of the great ironies of twentieth-century American politics is that Theodore Roosevelt, a fighting man to his marrow, the most bellicose individual ever to hold high public office in the United States, presided over seven years of *pax Americana.*

There *were* wars being fought during his presidency, but there seemed to be at least one reason in each a case for Roosevelt *not* to dispatch his military, to choose domestic leadership over foreign intervention. Which was even so in the case of an armed conflict abroad that he ended rather than joined.

The Russo-Japanese War, a contest of imperial ambitions over the nations of Manchuria and Korea, did not get much attention in the American press. The White House, however, watched it closely. Both Russia and Japan wanted to control their neighboring countries, the Russians largely because Port Arthur, in Manchuria, offered the warm-water port they so desperately needed; the Japanese largely because they coveted Manchuria's natural resources, iron and coal in particular, which they lacked within their own borders. As for Korea, it was simply close enough to Russia and Japan for them to think in terms of their own "manifest destiny" and annex it for sport.

Did Roosevelt consider military intervention, which would seem his natural impulse? There is no evidence of it, and one raises the question only because of what is known of him. In fact, far from taking up weapons,

Roosevelt assumed the role of arbitrator. With Japan spending money that it did not have on its military and the Russians suddenly more concerned about the prospects of a revolution at home than a friendly base for shipping overseas, Roosevelt faced little difficulty in brokering a truce.

The following year, he also arranged a truce between Germany and France, who were saber-rattling over Morocco.

Which led to an even greater irony. For his efforts in ending both the fighting and the rattling, Roosevelt won the Nobel Peace Prize in 1906. Theodore Roosevelt. The Nobel *Peace* Prize! It was a controversial choice, notes the Prize's website dryly, as Roosevelt was hardly known as a "peace apostle." It was as if Jesse James had put away his six-shooters and led the Sunday choir; as if Quenty-quee had earned a medal for decorum at Force.

There were few opportunities for Roosevelt to flex his muscles during his White House years. He could have assigned troops to Mexico, where there were already faint stirrings of the revolution that would erupt in 1910, eventually forcing President William Howard Taft to send 20,000 American soldiers south of the border. For now, though, the stirrings were *too* faint.

As for Angola, where the Portuguese military was in the process of suppressing a rebellion, and the French Congo, where native uprisings were becoming more and more common, Americans were indifferent. Besides, both places, like Russia and Japan, were too far away; U.S. troops could not be transported to such distant lands when they had so little at stake.

The closest that Roosevelt could come to battle was his dispatch of troops to Alaska when the United States and Canada were embroiled in a border dispute. But it was a minor matter, one that probably did not require a military presence at all. Roosevelt had overreacted, and members of both parties of Congress let him know about it. No shots were fired, and the dispute was eventually resolved by a tribunal. American troops executed a U-turn as soon as the orders came through.

The president also sent battleships to Panama in 1903, supporting that country's revolution against Colombia, and supporting all the more the canal being built at the time, which Americans correctly envisioned as a boon to both trade and Western settlement for them. The small fleet did not take part in the fighting; it was, rather, more of a demonstration that the Panamanians would have the United States behind them if they needed assistance. In other words, it was the same reason President McKinley had sent the *Maine* to Havana Harbor — for show.

Toward Cuba, the site of his lone military triumph, Roosevelt had changed his mind. By 1906, he had come to believe that the residents of the island nation were being insufficiently acquiescent to the whims of American rule. "I am so angry with that infernal little Cuban republic," Roosevelt once said, although behind closed doors, "that I would like to wipe its people off the face of the earth."

But it was not an option. He could not possibly go to war against a country when he had gone to war on its behalf less than a decade earlier, especially since that country had effectively been under U.S. control when the war ended. Furthermore, Cuba's various insubordinations, which at most got only a few lines in American newspapers, would have struck many of Roosevelt's countrymen as minor, perhaps even justified, examples that America was governing the island unfairly, too concerned with "manifesting its destiny." U.S. behavior was not nearly as cruel as Spain's had been;

nonetheless, the Cubans, under Roosevelt, remained a colonial subordinate, and that entailed occasional excesses in punishment. But those punishments could not be extended all the way to a military response.

You could almost hear the gnashing of teeth from behind the presidential desk.

Yet, when he wrote to Quentin, summering at Sagamore, he put his vexations aside, instead confessing an emotion he had never felt more achingly before.

Darling Quenty-quee: Slipper and the kittens are doing finely. I think the kittens will be big enough for you to pet and have some satisfaction out of when you get home, although they will be pretty young still. I miss you all dreadfully, and oh the [White] [H]ouse feels big and lonely and full of echoes with nobody but me in it; and I do not hear any small scamps running up and down the hall just as hard as they can; or hear their voices while I am dressing; or suddenly look out through the windows of the office at the tennis ground and see them racing over it or playing in the sand box. I love you very much. *Your loving father.*

Roosevelt did not like to be by himself, no

matter what the state of the world. He wanted his wife with him. He wanted his children. Most of all, he wanted his time with Quenty-quee.

In a manner of speaking, Roosevelt was able to go to battle domestically, finding his foe in the trusts, those vast and complex financial combinations created by monopolies to avoid the appearance of monopolizing. There were steel trusts, railroad trusts, banking trusts — none of them, in Roosevelt's opinion, deserving of public trust. They did not serve the greater good. They had begun to wreak havoc with justice in the marketplace before Roosevelt took office and would continue to do so, in ever more sophisticated guises, into the twenty-first century. For the most powerful monopolies, the real profits came before their products even reached the consumer, the result of (a) the control of all steps of production, from raw materials to finished goods, and (b) the mistreatment of the workingman: low wages, long hours, and inhumane conditions in dank, depressing, and even dangerous facilities.

"In no other country," Roosevelt fumed, ". . . was such power held by the men who had gained these fortunes. . . . The power of the mighty industrial overlords of the country had increased with great strides . . . the government [was] practically impotent. . . . Of all forms of tyranny, the least attractive and most vulgar is the tyranny of mere wealth, the tyranny of plutocracy."

Opposition to such tyranny made mortal enemies for Roosevelt out of some of the most legendary names in the country, such field generals of corporate greed as John D. Rockefeller, J. P. Morgan, Andrew Carnegie, Henry Clay Frick, Jay Gould, Edward Harriman, and the descendants of Cornelius Vanderbilt, a man of "superhuman stinginess," according to Mark Twain, who himself quotes Vanderbilt as admitting "I have been insane on the subject of money-making all my life." These were the so-called "robber barons," and to a man they felt betrayed by the president. Although they knew that Roosevelt did not come from inherited fortune, they also knew there were enough funds in the family vault so that he could be considered a member of the ruling elite, his present office notwithstanding. They felt he should have taken his place on the side of the fiscally gilded. By instead trying to protect the great majority of Americans who were wage slaves, he was, ipso facto, a traitor to his people.

It was precisely how the same kinds of men would react when Roosevelt's fifth cousin, Franklin Delano Roosevelt, became president and rained down upon them the countless, financially depleting programs of his New Deal.

Theodore didn't care. He fought the robber barons in court, in legislative chambers, in the press, and sometimes in face-to-face meetings, in his office, and even at social occasions. These men were "malefactors of great wealth," Roosevelt insisted, and he would not back down to them, would not yield in his quest for what he believed to be justice for their victims.

In fact, in 1902 he ordered the Justice Department to file suit against Morgan's Northern Securities, a trust so complicated and multi-tentacled that no one could figure out how many railroads it truly controlled, nor how many competitors it illegally drove into bankruptcy, nor how many millions of dollars it finagled out of customers by charging excessive rates for freight and personal transportation. No matter; the figures were high and so was public support for Roosevelt's position in the suit he had brought against Morgan's trust.

In 1904, he was victorious. In a surprising, yet narrow, five-to-four ruling, the

Supreme Court proclaimed that Northern Securities operated in restraint of trade, and should cease to exist, which it promptly did, shattered by judicial fiat into a number of smaller companies that struggled anew to find ways for illicit growth. It was the first antitrust case ever filed against a major monopoly and, despite having no precedent upon which to stand, Roosevelt stood supreme.

If his father were still hovering nearby, in whatever form he now assumed, he surely smiled down.

No less proud was Quentin. "Well, Father," he said, "I just saw a puzzle card with a picture of you whacking the trusts, and the motto 'We're for Teddy because Teddy protects the poor man.' " Quentin bought the card and kept it, a treasured souvenir.

Theodore continued to make his body during the White House years. His favorite sports were boxing and hunting. The former, even though it eventually cost him the sight in one eye, was apparently a means of letting off steam that he could not do without — especially now that he held the highest office in the land. To watch him in the ring was to see a man battling the constraints of duty as much as his flesh-

144

and-blood foe. He was often frustrated by the presidency's insufficiently dictatorial powers, its incomprehensibly bureaucratic requirements, all of the outside circumstances that stymied inner passions — and his sparring partner took the blows.

Hunting, of course, although dangerous, was a less punishing sport and, ultimately, a far more important part of his life. It was certainly not an ideal pastime for a man with darkening vision, but Roosevelt refused to be dissuaded and, given his handicap, was a skilled practitioner.

During both of his terms as president, and in fact beginning all the way back in 1886, Roosevelt and a few mates would refresh themselves from the demands of vocation by taking a few weeks off and heading for the Rockies or the Deep South. It did not matter where they were, in Minnesota or Arizona, Rhode Island or Kansas, even Europe — Paris, Rome, or London; they would put aside their professional responsibilities and live a life that was centuries old. No longer politicians or businessmen or academics, they were stalkers of wild beasts. They followed them through forest and plain and promontory, cornering them, firing for no other reason than the joy of the kill. It was, for Theodore, the missing piece of the complete man. "The qualities that make a good soldier," he wrote, "are, in large part, the qualities that make a good hunter. Most important of all is the ability to shift for oneself. . . . Skill in the use of the rifle is another trait; quickness in seeing game, another; ability to take advantage of cover, yet another; while patience, endurance, keenness of observation, resolution, good nerves, and instant readiness in an emergency, are all indispensable to a really good hunter."

Roosevelt wrote proudly to his wife about his 1886 sojourn to the American hinterlands, telling her that he "made a great bag, of two moose, a mountain bison, two bear and a cougar. One of the bears charged me in the most determined way." But he sidestepped the animal and then, taking aim, split his skull.

The animals Roosevelt brought down were his biggest haul to date, much more than he had amassed on a trip to Egypt with his mother and father when, as a boy of fourteen, he killed a solitary crane. But he could still remember picking it up, carrying it back to his parents, "eyes sparkling with delight." It was his first real success with a gun.

1886, though, was also the year that Theodore married Edith, and she was not happy that so little time had elapsed between the reciting of the vows and the loading of the firearms. Prior to her receiving the missive about the "great bag," she wrote, "It is four weeks tomorrow evening since you left, so more than half the wearying time has gone. . . . I miss you every minute, awake or asleep, and long for you beyond all expression."

Roosevelt began his replies to her plaints by calling her "DARLING EDIE," and telling her how much he loved her and how much her "dear, dear letters" meant to him. But he did not come home until he was ready to come home, and in fact went on in his own letters with an enthusiasm for his various quests that seemed to belittle her longing. He told her what creatures he had seen, what creatures he had shot, what fun it was to be miles from civilization with a rifle in hand and crisp, fresh air in his lungs. He told her how stimulating it was to know that perils lurked everywhere and could strike at any time, and that as a result all of his senses were on the alert, tingling. The feeling was incomparable. He also told her how invigorating it was to know that what he faced was the threats of real life, of nature, not the sneaky, artificial threats of political foes, starting with those in the New York Assembly, who were always plotting against him behind his back. He told her this year after year after year, all the way to the White House.

For instance, in 1907, from Louisiana: "I have seen one deer, running like a race horse through the cane; and by a lucky, and difficult shot I killed it . . . winning undeserved praise from all the party." He signed the letter, "YOUR OWN LOVER."

But he still did not come home, not from this hunt in particular. For 1907 was the next to last year of his presidency, and he had more nervous energy than usual to work off. He needed a few more rounds of ammunition than usual, a few more conquests. Edith had always understood, or at least forgiven, before. Theodore could not imagine her not reacting similarly now.

Oddly, although Roosevelt taught his oldest son Kermit how to shoot, he never taught Quentin. Yet the littlest Roosevelt delighted in the stories that his father brought back from his wildlife pursuits. They stimulated the boy's imagination but did not, apparently, create a passion. The passion was Theodore's, and Theodore's alone, and perhaps he wanted it that way — his own private blood lust, unknown to more than a few others.

In 1908, the last full year of the Roosevelt White House, he summoned the press corps for an announcement. "If a war should occur while I am still physically fit," he declared from the White House rostrum, apropos of absolutely nothing, "I should certainly try to raise a brigade of cavalry, mounted riflemen, such as those in my regiment ten years ago."

The reporters looked at one another in confusion. They had no idea what he meant. The president, it seemed, had just declared war against no one. How were they to write a story like that?

But by this time, Roosevelt and his advisers had already come up with the idea of the Great White Fleet. If the United States could not conquer at the present time, it could at least flaunt, showing off its naval fighting capacity in a round-the-world display of pomp and seamanship like nothing seen before or since. Claiming the seven seas as its own private parade route, an armada of U.S. Navy vessels set out from Hampton Roads, Virginia, on December 16, 1907 and returned to the same port on February 22, 1909, about two weeks before Roosevelt was to depart from the executive mansion.

The Great White Fleet was an assortment of sixteen U.S. battleships and twelve escorts, the name coming from the hulls of the ships, which had been painted so brightly that they virtually glowed, except for streaks of red and blue, added for patriotic display, at the bows. The purpose of the voyage was to circumnavigate the globe, for no other reason than that the President of the United States *could* command such a voyage. Theodore Roosevelt, who had been behaving with such uncharacteristic restraint in office, wanted to throw off his shackles and demonstrate the military man he was at heart. In the uncommonly bright twilight days of his administration, Roosevelt was determined to produce "a sheer pageant of power," a display of might that was the truth of the United States.

There was also a more practical reason for the pageant, although barely so, and we must take the president's word for it. According to a reliable source, he stated, neither the British nor the Germans thought America capable of an exhibition of seaborne might such as Roosevelt envisioned. There would be too much opposition in Congress, too much inefficiency among Naval officials, too much decrepitude in the U.S. armada. Roosevelt had to do something, he believed, to prove his doubters wrong. "Time to have a showdown in the matter," he is supposed to have said.

As the ships prepared to depart, Roosevelt stood on the pier at Hampton Roads and watched them glistening in the sunlight, the waves striking them and bouncing sharply back to shore. "Did you ever see such a fleet and such a day!" he exclaimed, forced to squint.

And, a few minutes later: "By George, isn't it magnificent!"

In the opinion of Rear Admiral Robley D. Evans, the Fleet's commander, expressed earlier to Roosevelt, his men were ready for "a feast, a frolic or a fight."

When the Fleet passed American shores, hundreds of thousands of people showed up in random locations to wave their arms and flags and shout hurrah. When it sailed along the Australian coast, it became a rallying point for those who wanted their country to create a navy of its own. When it cruised into Yokohama, Japan, the crews of the U.S. vessels gave in to pleas to disembark and walk past thousands of joyous schoolchildren waving their flags so energetically that they almost seemed like weapons. Disembarking again in Sicily, American sailors helped in relief efforts after an earthquake several months earlier, the men demonstrating heart as well as courage. The Great White Fleet, according to the consensus of American newspapers, was great in a multitude of ways.

After more than a year, fifteen glorious months of American bravado at sea, the president stood on the bridge of a new presidential yacht called the *Mayflower,* a top hat on his head to mark the formality of the occasion, and watched the Great White Fleet arise slowly over the horizon and return to Hampton Roads, the boats seeming to some even whiter than they had been upon departure, illuminated by icy winter skies. "That is the answer to my critics," the president said. "Another chapter is complete, and I could not ask a finer concluding scene for my administrations."

15

But the statement raises a question, one of great historical importance, never satisfactorily answered. It is, simply: Why? For what reason was the end of the Fleet's voyage the conclusion to Roosevelt's reign? For what reason had he determined to leave office so soon after the ships had returned? He did not have to. He had not been elected to the presidency twice, having served a first term of three years-plus as a result of McKinley's assassination. Roosevelt could have run again in 1908 with minimal controversy, if any at all, and would easily have won — which means that, by not running, Roosevelt denied a majority of the electorate the chance to vote for the man they most wanted to lead them. And in the process, in no way that can ever be discerned, he changed the entire course of the American future.

But not only had he refused another term, he had done so four years earlier. In 1904, after having easily beaten the Democratic challenger, Judge Alton B. Parker, Roosevelt announced that he would not be a candidate in the next election, referring to "[t]he wise custom which limits the President to two terms." It was a custom that dated back to George Washington; far be it from Theodore Roosevelt to deny it. He swore that "under no circumstances will I be a candidate for or accept another nomination."

The declaration was clear, decisive. It was not, however, an explanation. Rather, it was a begging of the question. Why had he come to such a conclusion in the first place? Why so early? And why did he believe that, as the Constitution defined the term, he had already served two *full* terms? In fact, according to the Constitution's definition, he had not. He was yielding, as he said, to custom, not law, and even a custom set in place by so eminent a figure as George Washington carried no legal standing.

As far as his wife was concerned, his wife who so seldom offered opinions about her husband's political affairs, it was the worst decision he ever made. Theodore "tied with his tongue," Edith cleverly stated, a knot he "could not undo with his teeth."

But, when he announced his non-candidacy, it was still early. There was plenty of time between 1904 and 1908 for him to change his mind. Those who supported him were still left with the hope that he would do just that, and those who were close to him, who had his ear, were ceaseless with their urgings.

In 1908, though, he was no less determined than before not to seek the presidency, and he finally got around to an explanation. Of a sort. "New issues are coming up," he told a reporter. "I see them. People are going to discuss economic issues more and more: the tariff, currency, banks. They are hard questions, and I am not deeply interested in them: my problems are moral problems, and my teaching has been plain morality."

With this, many of his supporters gave up. They believed him now, and were confused and disappointed, some even angry. He was letting down the party. He was letting down the country. Roosevelt heard it time and again.

His youngest son was not happy either.

In 1908, the day after the Republican convention came to a close, the convention that chose William Howard Taft as its presidential nominee, that heard but did not heed chorus after chorus of "Draft Roosevelt" pleadings, Theodore, who had not attended the festivities, was chatting with Quentin in one of the White House rooms. All seemed normal until, suddenly, the boy turned quiet. He would not speak even in response to his father's comments. Roosevelt studied him for a long moment, thought about asking what was bothering him. He decided, however, that it would be better to wait out the boy. It took only a few more seconds.

"There is a little hole in my stomach," Quentin admitted, in something close to a whisper, "when I think of leaving the White House."

Alice was even more upset. Before moving

out of her grand residence, she constructed and then buried a voodoo doll of Mrs. Taft beneath the lawn. The new First Lady, Alice had apparently decided, belonged in the Executive Mansion no more than her stepmother did.

Many years afterward, Earle Looker, mourning the end of the White House Gang that broke up with Roosevelt's departure, took a more mature view, realizing that "somehow, the old days of joyously rioting behavior had gone forever. For one thing, we were growing older, and, in some very important aspects, the Gang just naturally died when the small boy, in each of us, gave place to one of a larger, less spontaneous age and mould. But the story was by no means ended. As a matter of plain fact, it was no end at all, but a beginning, for Quentin and for us all."

16

Roosevelt and Taft were not friends of long standing. Rather, they had formed a bond largely because Roosevelt was impressed with Taft's work as Governor-General of the Philippines, despite the occasional native uprisings. His "high-mindedness stood him always in good stead," Roosevelt believed,

". . . and he was able to enjoy a notable success during his four years" of governance in the Pacific.

Actually, Taft spent some of those years elsewhere, running errands for the president in such far-flung locales as Cuba; Japan; Panama, before the fighting broke out with Colombia, to assure the Panamanians that it was only the canal we wanted, not their country; and the Vatican, to buy some land that the Church owned in the Philippines, where our intention was to grab even more territory than we had already usurped. Roosevelt was pleased with Taft's handling of all these chores, and was beginning to feel a special kind of bond with him.

As a result, Taft was summoned to Washington to serve as Secretary of War. It was more than just a political appointment; it was as if Roosevelt had created a new Cabinet post, a Secretary of Bonhomie. There was something about the way the two men behaved toward each other, something one would not expect from people in their positions, a kind of closeness that came about quickly and suddenly, and that even those who did not know them well could notice. Perhaps, as has been speculated, "Taft became for Roosevelt something of a younger brother (although Taft was actually the older of the two by a year). It was almost as though Roosevelt, having lost Elliott a decade before and never having discovered a replacement, now turned to Taft."

When the two men discussed politics, they discovered they were brothers in ideas. To some, in fact, the similarity of their thoughts was disturbing. Theodore's wife was among them. "They are too much alike," Edith said and, although she could not have explained why, she was apprehensive.

As it turned out, they were not as alike as she thought. Edith was right to feel apprehensive, just not for the right reason.

The relationship was one-sided; both men wanted it to be. The dominant Roosevelt admired Taft's intelligence, valued his thoughtful ways, and took great pleasure in his willingness to be bullied. The buoyantly deferential Taft respected Roosevelt's self-confidence, envied his energy and candor, and happily acceded to his own need to serve such a man. Although, as Roosevelt would soon learn, that need did have its limits.

As the pair of them grew ever closer, it became obvious that Taft would be Roosevelt's choice to succeed him. Taft was dubious at first, having hoped for a seat on the Supreme Court. Roosevelt, however, would not be denied. He urged Taft to take up residence in the White House with a barrage of compliments. "You cannot know," he said to Taft on one occasion, "how absolutely you have the trust and confidence of all our people whose trust and confidence are best worth having." There were more statements, many more, of a similar kind. All positives, no negatives, even though Roosevelt knew that others were dubious about Taft and he was already mulling over their reservations. But even with his own reservations, Taft found it impossible to resist a suitor who wooed so persuasively and often.

Still, Roosevelt had lost none of his perceptiveness. He knew that he and the object of his affection were different in a very important way: the impression they made on others. Roosevelt was a dynamo. Taft, although jovial at times, was more often timid — the most recalcitrant and unimposing 332-pound human being in the history of American public life. Because of his heft, he also achieved a lesser distinction: he is the only person ever to have gotten stuck in the White House bathtub, a mishap that required a battery of assistants to pry him out, creating a sound that was like a champagne cork being popped out of a bottle. The incident would result, a century later, in a children's book called *President Taft Is Stuck in the Bath*.

Roosevelt's popularity, however, was such that anyone he endorsed for the Republican nomination would have won the presidency. Taft accomplished the feat without effort, giving the Democrat, William Jennings Bryan, yet one more defeat. It was, in fact, the most decisive, and last, of Bryan's three losses for the nation's highest office. It was also, in Roosevelt's opinion, the next best thing to winning re-election himself.

Taft assumed the presidency on March 4, 1909. By this time, Roosevelt was more willing to acknowledge the negatives, and on Inauguration Day he was unable to resist a display of his misgivings. "Observers were struck by Roosevelt's immobile concentration," according to one report, "as his successor was sworn in. Those who did not know him thought that the stony expression and balled-up fists signaled trouble ahead for Taft." And, in fact, they did. Although it was an action Taft had himself taken that so severely upset Theodore. Shortly before the inauguration, the soon-to-be ex-president had learned that Taft would dismiss most of

Roosevelt's Cabinet officers and bring in a staff of his own. And he would take so drastic a step without even consulting his predecessor. As if he had a mind of his own — a trait that he had not revealed previously in his relations with Roosevelt, and the absence of which had appealed to Theodore greatly. In fact, it was not good politics, or even good manners, for Taft to announce a housecleaning before even taking possession of the house; it would justifiably have upset even someone less volatile than Roosevelt.

When the ceremony was over, Roosevelt wedged his high hat onto his head and walked away, speaking to no one, looking at no one. Walked away, in fact, with his fists still balled up. It was said that quite a few people in the throng attending the ceremony, seeing the man they still thought of as president depart from the White House, began to weep.

The only member of the Roosevelt family to stay for the parade following the official change of power was Quentin, sitting with his White House Gang pal Taffy, the two of them making the best of things, laughing and joking with each other but forcing it, knowing they were about to go their separate ways. Knowing also that, because of

their fathers' change of roles, their friendship would never be the same. The hole in
Quentin's stomach grew larger.

17

As far as Roosevelt was concerned, the
question now was what to do with himself.
Even before Taft started parading along
Pennsylvania Avenue that afternoon, waving
at the hordes of largely unenthusiastic
people lining his route, he realized a problem lay ahead that he had never anticipated.
Still hearty and opinionated — he remains,
after all this time, the youngest person ever
to have served as president and was a
stripling of fifty when he gave up the office
— he could not stash himself away at
Sagamore Hill. He could not take up residence anywhere in New York, nor, in fact,
anywhere in the United States. And it was
not just because of his age and unquench-
able vitality.

If he remained in the country, especially
during the period when Taft was first ac-
customing himself to life as chief executive,
Roosevelt would be seen as his puppet
master, a political "boss" of a sort. And
Taft's attempts to rise to presidential stature
on his own merits would be undermined,
Roosevelt's very proximity ensuring that.

162

Both men, then, would be diminished in the public eye. So, Theodore could see no choice but to exile himself for a time, allowing Taft the space he needed, hoping that the dismemberment of his Cabinet was not the portent it seemed and that the new administration would prove to be, as Roosevelt had intended all along, an extension of his own.

But where was the previous incumbent to go? What was he to do?

The answer came to him in a flash. Africa. A safari. Yes, of course, a *safari*! What kind of excursion could be more fitting for a man of arms in a world at peace? This would not be like tramping through the Rockies. This would not be navigating through swampland in Louisiana. This would be the ultimate hunting trip, the best of all possible reasons to leave his home behind. "By George," he wrote to a friend, "I am as eager to go to Africa and to hunt . . . as a boy who has been reading dime novels and wishes to go West and fight Indians."

Roosevelt would dispatch himself to the jungles of the dark continent, where he would not only be removed from American politics, but armed for battle against the fiercest creatures in the world — much more than those still-annoying Cubans. He would be back at war, so to speak, but would be constantly on the move. Meaning that reporters, of whom he had grown weary after their endless questioning of his decision not to run, would be unable to track him down, badger him for opinions about Taft's performance. He would not *know* about Taft's performance. Ignorance would be bliss.

The more he thought about it, the more fervid he became. To Roosevelt, "there are no words that can tell the hidden spirit of the wilderness, that can reveal its mystery, its melancholy, and its charm. There is delight in the hardy life of the open, in long rides with rifles in hand, in the thrill of the fight with dangerous game. Apart from this, yet mingled with it, is the strong attraction . . . of the large tropic moons, and the splendor of the new stars; where the wanderer sees the awful glory of sunrise and sunset in the wide waste spaces of the earth, unworn of man, and changed only by the slow change of the ages through time everlasting."

On Roosevelt's first full day out of Washington and temporarily back at Sagamore Hill, reporters and photographers swarmed the grounds, hoping that the lord of the manor would step outside and give his first impressions of life as a private citizen, a position he had not held for two decades. He did indeed make an appearance, but only to ask the members of the Fourth Estate to remove themselves from his property. "Gentlemen," he said, not even opening his front door all the way, "I do not wish you to think I am churlish. This seems like giving you the marble heart, but I have nothing to say and am not going to give interviews to anyone. Also I will not stand for any more photographs." And with that, he disappeared back into the house and started the lengthy planning for what he thought of as the trek of a lifetime.

The safari was to last a year. It was a long time, the longest ever for him to be away from the family he so loved. But Roosevelt's excitements tended to overpower his common sense, as had been the case with the length of his domestic hunting trips and Edith's dismay at both his absence and the activity that occasioned them. During the lengthy period of planning and gathering funds and equipment for the safari, he allowed his family to recede into the background, even though his wife and children began missing him as soon as he announced the safari. More than that, they felt a degree of confusion, at times even resentment, as they watched him bustle in and out of the house, enthusiastically preparing for a venture that would exclude them for so long a period. He seemed, in fact, to be excluding them from his life even now, so single-mindedly was he envisioning life in Africa.

Only Kermit was spared a sense of alienation. At nineteen, he was both old enough and, unlike Ted, skilled enough as a marksman to accompany his father; in addition, he had had training as an engineer. He, too, bustled in and out of Sagamore, returning with backpacks and headgear, maps and guidebooks, almost as eager to take a year off from college as he was to spend that year on the greatest hunt of his life.

The rest of the family, however, could not share in Theodore's and Kermit's excitement, and the result was an uncommon degree of tension in the household, an increasingly depressive atmosphere as the day for departure approached. But the child within Roosevelt, as selfish and short-sighted as all children can be, did not notice such things, and in fact they would not even flicker in his mind until he was actually climbing up the gangplank, boarding the ship that would take him to another world. Then, all of a sudden, he would be struck by the specter of his coming loneliness as if it were a shock to him, something apparent only as he took in the immensity of the ship, itself another world. Now it was his turn to contribute to — and increase — the household tension. He would not be there for it, of course, but he would feel his own share. He was that six-year-old, as someone once called him, finally aware of something he should have known from the start.

Financing for the safari would come from two sources. First were advances that Roosevelt had received for the writing he would do about his travels, most of which would appear as articles in *Scribner's* magazine and would later be collected, rewritten, and expanded on for a book to be called *African Game Trails.*

The second source was donations from a number of individuals, including Andrew Carnegie, with whom he had quickly made amends now that his trust-busting days were over and a fund-seeking mission had arisen in its place. Carnegie, in the philanthropic phase of his life now, was especially attracted to the enterprise, as Roosevelt had promised both the Smithsonian Institution in Washington and the Museum of Natural History in New York — of which his father had been one of the founders and Carnegie had been the principal figure in its achieving world-class eminence — that he would bring back numerous specimens for them, both to display and study. He would, of course, be true to his word. Too true, as far as some people were concerned.

Roosevelt appointed himself commander-in-chief of the expedition. Kermit, not yet showing the effects of depression and alcohol that would so torment him in later years, would be second in command. Two guides, known as white hunters, were hired, and the guides would arrange for porters and other logistical matters when they got to Africa.

Quentin pleaded to go with his father, but Roosevelt would not hear of it. A safari was too dangerous an undertaking for someone who had so far accumulated a mere eleven years.

Quentin, of course, did not take the decision passively. He reminded his father that, with Admiral Rixey's help, he had gone hunting for the first time not long ago and ended the lives of three rabbits. He had plucked them out of the puddles of their blood, wiped them as best he could against bushes and tree trunks, and toted them home, proudly displaying them to his father, who was himself so proud that he wrote about the occasion, describing his son as "very dirty and very triumphant."

But Roosevelt gently pointed out to Quentin that he and his men would face no animals as gentle as rabbits once they arrived in Africa — and that, as far as the boy's importuning went, was that. The hole in Quentin's stomach could only have grown.

Roosevelt promised he would write, though, not only to Quentin but to everyone in the family. He would write to people out of the family. He would write his magazine articles, take additional notes for *African Game Trails*. He would fill notebook after notebook, stationery page after stationery page, setting down his thoughts about the safari and the longing he felt for those he had left behind. But it was also important for them to know how important his African experiences would be as a catharsis, a rejuvenation, his grand farewell to American politics, a great white fleet of the terra firma. "I shall not be more than half satisfied if there are bullets other than my own in the animals that I kill," he proclaimed. "I don't intend to go into this as a sham."

There would be others' bullets in the

safari's victims, too, many of them. But Roosevelt would end up being just as satisfied as he had hoped.

In the late spring of 1909, with the ex-president having been out of office only a few weeks, with his teary insistence to Quentin that he be a good boy slightly more than a week behind him, and with his plans in order to meet an equally teary Edith in Egypt in March 1910, Roosevelt and his companions boarded their ship, the *Hamburg,* in Hoboken, New Jersey.

Entering his cabin, Theodore found a letter from Taft awaiting him on the bed. He picked it up reluctantly, shaking his head. He did not want to look at it, did not want to think about whatever it was that Taft was thinking about.

Tearing open the envelope, he read the following:

If I followed my impulse I should still say "My dear Mr. President," I cannot overcome the habit. When I am addressed as "Mr. President" I turn to see whether you are not at my elbow. When I read in the newspaper of a conference between the Speaker and the President, or between Senator Aldrich and the

President, I wonder what the subject of the conference was, and can hardly identify the report with the fact that I had a talk with the two gentlemen. . . .

Many questions have arisen since the Inauguration with respect to which I should like to have consulted you, but I have forborne to interrupt your well-earned quiet and to take up your time when it must have been so much occupied with preparation for your long trip. . . .

I want you to know that I do nothing in the Executive Office without considering what you would do under the same circumstances and without having in a sense a mental talk with you over the pros and cons of the situation.

Roosevelt must have read the message with mixed emotions. On the one hand, he would have been pleased at Taft's reassurance that he would dance to the strings that his predecessor manipulated offstage. On the other, he must have cringed at the tone of the writing. It was not assertive, not . . . manly. Roosevelt always thought of Taft as a subordinate, although perhaps not to the extent he showed here; here he was like a beggar at court, seeking favor, uncertain how deeply to bow in the process. But Roosevelt wrote back and encouraged his man as best he could. He sent the letter off to the White House, then vowed to himself to forget about both the contents and the recipient for as long as he could.

Still, he might have thought, if only in passing, that it was as if he had become to Taft not what brother Elliott had once been to him, but what the ghost of Theodore, Senior continued to be.

The ocean passage was smooth, the unruly camaraderie of those on the ship in vivid contrast to the vast, enveloping solitude of the sea. Once they arrived in British East Africa, today known as Kenya, and took a day or two to recuperate, Theodore, out for a stroll, found himself in the presence of a baby gazelle. He asked for a bottle, fed the animal, then wrote to Quentin about it that very evening. It was his first letter home. Things were about to get a lot less chummy between Roosevelt and the denizens of the jungle, and Quentin knew it as well as Theodore. Still, envisioning the scene must have brought the little boy pleasure, as did the speed with which his father's first missive had reached him. Quentin quickly spread the word around Sagamore, proud of being the initial possessor of a report from Africa.

The rest period having ended, Roosevelt and company set out from the city of Mombasa in search of a pride of lions, riding a rickety railway for 600 miles to the Belgian Congo, since become the Democratic Republic of the Congo. Roosevelt actually did some of his riding on the train's cowcatcher, "on an observation bench rigged for him. . . . He has the delightful illusion of being transported into the Pleistocene Age."

No less delightful was the reality. He was at last in game country. "At one time," Roosevelt would state in *African Game Trails,* "we passed a herd of a dozen or so great giraffes, sows and calves, cantering along through the open woods a couple of hundred yards to the right of the train. Again, still closer, four waterbuck cows, their big ears thrown forward, stared at us without moving until we had passed. Hartebeests were everywhere; one herd was on the track, and when the engine whistled they bucked and sprang with ungainly agility, galloping clear of the danger."

But there was no shooting, not yet, only sightseeing, and the scenery was spectacular. So were Roosevelt's descriptions of it. "The track shot across plains shimmering in the heat," then "climbed escarpments into the clouds, dropped vertiginously into flowered forests, and leapt swamp and gorge." Roosevelt was "enchanted" by it all. The sun was set to low-bake and the grassy, lush green grass of the plains sparkled like emeralds under a spotlight.

At the end of the rail line, the hunters were surprised by their reception. It was not just lions that awaited them, but a multitude of other species: giraffes, zebras, oryxes, elephants, gazelles, cheetahs, impalas, and the most unexpected and unwanted species of all — journalists!

Mr. President, what do you think of Taft's decision to do this?
What about his decision to do that?
How do you think he's filling your shoes?
Should he send troops to Mexico?
Would you like to lead a brigade?
Do you think there'll be a revolution?
Mr. President, has Taft got what it takes?
Mr. President, Mr. President. . . .

His impulses perhaps to the contrary, Roosevelt would fire his weapons only at the animals.

He was, of course, hampered by his lessening vision in one eye. As a result, he showed more persistence with his gun than he did accuracy. "Sometimes I shot fairly well," he wrote home, "and sometimes badly. On one day, for instance, the entry in my diary ran: 'Missed steinbuck ["steenbok," a small antelope], pig, impala and Grant; awful.' On another day it ran in part as follows: 'Out with [naturalist Edmund] Heller. Hartebeest, 250 yards, facing me, shot through face, broke neck. Zebra, very large, quartering, 160 yards, between neck and shoulder. Buck Grant, 220 yards, walking, behind shoulder. Steinbuck, 180 yards, standing, behind shoulder.' Generally each head of game bagged cost me a goodly number of bullets; but only twice did I wound animals which I failed to get."

Although the porters did the actual work, Theodore and Kermit oversaw the shipping of their prey back to the United States. The Smithsonian and the Museum of Natural History welcomed delivery after delivery, crate after crate. It was, to them, treasure chest after treasure chest.

To members of animal-rights groups, however, it was coffin after coffin. The groups, already in existence, as well as individuals who had long opposed Roosevelt because of his apparent bloodthirst in human affairs, were appalled by the museums' forthcoming exhibits. They held public meetings to protest the murder of innocent creatures, wrote letters to the museums as well as to newspapers denouncing the safari, and pleaded with friends of Roosevelt as well as to prominent editorial writers and other opinion-makers to urge him to stop.

He did not. He never even considered it. His defense, as was his way, was to take the offensive, accusing those who criticized him of being panty-waists and, worse, hypocrites. These were the very people, Roosevelt charged, who would go to the Smithsonian and marvel at the displays, the very people who would attend the Museum of Natural History and stand in front of the stuffed animals for which he was responsible and teach their children about the splendors of African wildlife. His expedition, he boomed from afar, would advance scientific knowledge, stir curiosity, and increase interest in conserving natural habitats. To condemn his safari, Roosevelt believed, was to condemn two of the finest institutions of learning in all the United States. It was, in fact, to condemn the very idea of learning. Case closed, as far as Roosevelt was concerned.

The safari proceeded onward.

Theodore Roosevelt, as a Rough Rider in the Spanish-American War, which made him a national hero yet left him oddly disappointed. The war, he complained, was too short, and was in fact the shortest in American history.

Roosevelt, wearing glasses, stands proudly in the midst of his fellow Rough Riders, warriors all.

ABOVE: A sketch of President William McKinley's assassination, which elevated vice president Roosevelt, a controversial choice even among fellow Republicans, to the nation's highest office. BELOW: Theodore Roosevelt being sworn in as president. At the age of 42, he was the youngest man ever to assume the White House.

LEFT: Lincoln Steffens, a great American journalist, was disturbed by Roosevelt's frank conversations with him upon assuming the presidency. But he kept his doubts to himself. BELOW: The president, whose pen sometimes *was* his sword, at work.

TOP: The Great White Fleet, which sailed the world in 1907–8, Roosevelt's pointlessly grandiose display of American naval power, which brought his tenure of chief executive to an end. CENTER: The Great White Hunter, Roosevelt at ease in Africa, having fled from the United States to spend a year on safari after yielding the White House. RIGHT: William Howard Taft, who, having been Roosevelt's hand-picked successor as chief executive, was also supposed to have been his puppet. A gentle man, Taft was forced into a transit from Roosevelt's friend to bitter enemy, and it broke his heart.

President Woodrow Wilson, who denied Roosevelt the opportunity to join his sons in World War I, finding him too old, and perhaps too full of himself. Besides, Wilson despised Roosevelt as much as Roosevelt despised Wilson.

ABOVE: [exterior of Roosevelt House] And so, denied a final chance to be a fighting man, Roosevelt had little to do in his last years but spend time at his home, Sagamore Hill in Oyster Bay, New York.

CENTER AND BOTTOM LEFT: The interior of Sagamore Hill reveals its squire as clearly as any house ever reflected the personality of its occupant. BOTTOM RIGHT: Flora Payne Whitney, a frequent visitor to Sagamore Hill, one of the wealthiest young women in America, who wanted nothing more in life than to be Mrs. Quentin Roosevelt.

That summer, Quentin also crossed the Atlantic. It was his first trip abroad, and he was accompanied by his mother and Archie. Their destination was France, Quentin having long since mastered the language and, more recently, through his reading, developed an appreciation for the country's culture and amusements. The three Roosevelts landed in Avignon on August 5. They added to their group a Swiss maid and, after a short time, subtracted Archie, who had been invited to join the American ambassador to France on a separate journey. Edith and Quentin would meet him later in Lyon.

Meanwhile, mother and youngest son spent some time in Avignon taking in the sights and attending the theatre. Among the former, it was the Palais de Papes that engaged Quentin most. A former home to the Papacy, medieval Gothic in style and more than two and a half acres in size, the Palais was a building whose towers soared on the outside and, with its magnificent vaulting, dazzled the eye inside. Never before had Quentin seen beauty on such a scale. He was constantly looking upward. He could not express its effect on him except to say that, somehow, it made him want to be free, to be a bird that could circle the tops of the towers and then ascend from there, disappearing high above the horizon. He might have been regretting the starlings he had brought to earth several years ago.

He and Edith next traveled to Paris, where Quentin dug into his trunk for "a bully camera, a 1-A Kodak," with which he took pictures of everything that caught his eye, and in the French capital so much did. He sent most of the photos to his siblings. He also shared his impressions with them, such letter-writers these Roosevelts were. He informed them that he and his mother "have had a wonderful time here and seen lots. We were at Rhems [Rheims] and saw all the aeroplanes flying, and saw Curtis [Curtiss] who won the Gordon Bennett cup [Cup] for swiftest flight. You don't know how pretty it was to see all the aeroplanes sailing at a time. At one time there were 4 aeroplanes in the air. It was the prettiest thing I ever saw. The prettiest one of the ones was a monoplane called the Antoinette, which looks like a great big bird in the air — it does not wiggle at all and goes very fast. It is awfully pretty turning."

Just as something about the churches made Quentin think of birds in flight, so did something about the aeroplanes make him think about the holy spires, straining to reach the celestial realms through which the aeroplanes now soared.

As far as history knows, his letters from Rheims were Quentin's first recorded paeans to flight. It would turn out to be the most important passion of his life.

But more than aircraft, it was the art and architecture of Paris that inspired Quentin at present. "Isn't Notre Dame wonderful? I think anything could be religious in it. And the Louvre, I think it would take at least a year to see it. I have some of the pictures. I think the little Infanta Margarita by Velazquez is the cunningest thing I ever saw, and I think they are all very beautiful. We have been to Rouen and everywhere."

Later, he and his mother visited yet another famed cathedral, this at Chartres, where he lit a candle "and said a little prayer to whatever power looks after those who have been separated when love and life were sweetest." He had had so much fun with his father when he was younger; perhaps he was thinking of the time they were not spending together now. He was still, after all, only a child, not yet in his teens. He missed his big, gruff playmate.

19

Ultimately, Theodore and Kermit and their companions ended up being disappointed in the Belgian Congo; the hunting was not as good as they had hoped and the heat was like a tangible object through which they had to make their way, the air nearly as dense as the jungle vegetation itself. Better luck, however, awaited them as they paddled up the Nile toward the Sudan, and in fact when they got there Roosevelt finally brought down a giant eland, his own personal Moby Dick, an animal that he had dreamed of many times but never before encountered. "The pointed bullet from the little Springfield," Roosevelt wrote, "hit [the eland] a trifle too far back and up, but made such a rip that he never got ten yards from where he was standing; and great was my pride as I stood over him, and examined his horns, twisted almost like a koodoos [a large African antelope, properly spelled 'kudu'], and admired his size, his finely modeled head and legs, and the beauty of his coat."

Theodore and Kermit and the rest of the gamesmen spent several weeks prowling through the Sudan's savannas and undergrowths. They were firing all the way — speaking softly, carrying big sticks, and expelling bullets from them at a prodigious rate. The porters toted wooden boxloads of ammunition when the safari began, struggling with the weight of them; there was virtually nothing left when the trip finally came to an end.

In fact, the total number of animals that Roosevelt and his mates either killed, trapped, or otherwise captured in Africa is believed to be 11,397, and included creatures as tiny as insects and as mammoth as hippopotamuses, elephants, and, among the rarest of African wildlife, the white rhino. In addition, he and Kermit and the others bagged "11 elephants, 20 [other] rhinoceroses, 9 giraffes, 47 gazelles, 8 hippopotamuses, 29 zebras, 9 hyenas, and a scattering of such odd creatures as the bongo, the dik-dik, the kuku, the aardwolf, and the klipspringer."

The totals were impressive. But they could easily have been higher, Roosevelt believed, and he taunted those who opposed the safari by pointing out his restraint. "We were in hunting grounds practically as good as any that have ever existed," he wrote; "but we did not kill a tenth, nor a hundredth part of what we might have killed had we been willing."

As for the Smithsonian and the Museum of Natural History, they were beyond inundated, so many shipments of animals having descended on them, so much more than they had expected, that it took several years for them just to be catalogued and studied, much less put on display. And even then the two institutions would find themselves with so many specimens left over that they were able to share Roosevelt's bounty with other museums around the country.

Scientists were appreciative not only of this largesse but of the care that Roosevelt and his men took in recording the locations and circumstances of their kills, in addition to carefully labeling the animals and parts of their anatomy for further examination. The support of the scientific community was further rebuttal, Roosevelt believed, to all those animal-rights whiners who, in his view, were not campaigning for animal rights at all, but for ignorance of the world around them.

20

The time had finally come for Quentin to leave the nest. Back in the United States after his summer abroad, the last of the Roosevelt children amazed the family, possibly even himself, by winning a scholarship to Groton. It was front-page news in the *New York Times.* Of course, he had been enrolled since birth; but, the scholarship notwithstanding, he would come to wish he hadn't been. The school might have been a prestigious one, and a jumping-off point to Harvard for his brothers, but Quentin quickly determined that he did not like the place, anything about it. "Latin is awful," he reported, and he found English troublesome; as for life outside the classroom, it was "dull, very dull." According to one letter he sent to his Aunt Ethel, the only break in the routine he managed to find was illness, a cough sending him to bed for a few days and thus giving him time to catch up on his correspondence.

He also wrote to Ethel about something that happened when he got over his cough, something embarrassing beyond tolerance. She was the only one he told.

After taking a shower following gym class, he found that one of his classmates had taken his towel. Spotting the thief, he immediately gave chase. The former ran outside; the latter followed closely. The problem was that the thief was clothed and his pursuer was not. The thief ran toward the main campus and Quentin, attired in his birthday suit and not a stitch more, ran after him, later claiming he was so intent on reclaiming his towel that he momentarily forgot his bare-skinned condition.

But one cannot remain in such a state for long, no matter how powerfully he focuses on another matter. Suddenly, Quentin looked down at himself and jammed on his brakes in embarrassment. He looked around, saw no one nearby. With his hands assuming the traditional fig-leaf position, he bolted back for the gym at the greatest speed he had ever attained. But someone had locked the door. He had no choice but to run around to the opposite side of the building and enter through the front doors, which he knew would be open during daylight hours. He took refuge inside the building as fast as he could, leaning against the wall, gasping in embarrassment more than enervation.

But he had not really found refuge. Rather, he had found even further humiliation — for no sooner had he re-entered the gym and found himself in the lobby, the building's main gathering place, than he realized his presence had interrupted a group of women taking a tour of the campus, their visit now including a naked student standing directly in front of them and gulping in humiliation. One might imagine the looks on their faces — and *his*! One might imagine the sound of the women's own gasping, and the haste with which dozens of pairs of eyes snapped shut, an action taken so unanimously that it, too, might have been audible. And one might imagine the silent vows the women took that — Harvard's reputation be cursed! — they would never send *their* sons to a school that enrolled such libertines as the flummoxed young man before them.

At present, Quentin wrote, concluding his letter to Ethel, he was waiting "in fear & trembling" for the headmaster to discipline him. He feared, but did not receive, the worst. He seems instead to have been given a scathing lecture, fueled by the shameful lengths to which he had gone to retrieve his towel, but tempered somewhat by sympathy for its removal from his locker. He was not suspended, not expelled, not even put on probation — only cautioned to be sure he was clothed whenever he stepped outdoors in the future.

He promised he would be.

It is not known what Quentin did when he finally found the towel thief.

He was, by this time, approaching the look of manhood, specifically his father's variety thereof, as he was "[b]ig of brow and burly bodied, forever baring his teeth in fits of laughter." For several years now, he had been a "freakish duplication" of his father in other ways. As biographer Edmund Morris put it, Quentin, like his father, had a "queer, prudish chivalry. (When classmates giggled at a girl's up-folded dress, he yanked it down, trembling with anger.) He had the same physical courage, clarity of perception, and ability to concentrate totally on any task at hand. Yet, more than any of the other Roosevelt children except Alice — who in any case had a different mother — he had a large personality of his own."

That personality reached a peak of jolliness with the approach of Christmas during his first year at Groton, when he was sprung from prison, as he thought of it, and allowed to return to Sagamore Hill. One day over the break, with the weather as mild as he could ever remember its having been at this time of year, he wandered outside and climbed the 70-foot windmill, next to the house, that pumped water into an underground reservoir. From the top he could see the town of Oyster Bay and hundreds of miles around it — a spectacular view, an unearthly quiet except for the whisper of breezes. His mother, discovering him in so precarious a position, was horrified. She screamed at him to get down. He grinned at her and waved. It was just like being a kid again. Or still.

Except that when he was a kid, his father was around for Christmas. He had never missed one before. Sagamore Hill was not the same place without him.

21

Theodore was feeling the ache of absence himself. In February 1910, with the safari not yet over and another month looming before he would see Edith in Cairo, Roosevelt found himself lonelier, wearier, and perhaps filthier than he had ever been before. "I want to go home!" he wrote. "I am homesick for my own land and my own people! Of course it is Mrs. Roosevelt I most want to see; but I want to see my two youngest boys; I want to see my own house, my own books and trees, the sunset over the sound from the window in the north room, the people with whom I have worked, who think my thoughts and speak my speech."

He also wanted to go home because, try though he did to isolate himself from the world of American politics, occasional bits of news managed to get through to him, and their implications were ominous. It seemed that President Taft was having difficulty governing. After the letter that had awaited him upon his occupying the *Hamburg,* Roosevelt did not hear from Taft again until the safari was almost over. "It is now near a year and three months since I assumed office," Taft wrote in the new missive, "and I have had a hard time. I do not know that I have had harder luck than other presidents, but I do know that thus far I have succeeded far less than have others. I have been conscientiously trying to carry out your policies but my method of doing so has not worked smoothly."

The reason for Taft's ineffectiveness, Roosevelt knew and should have known all along, was simple: he was not Roosevelt. Taft tried to reason with legislators, and when that didn't work he attempted bargaining and sometimes even begging. But he could not put his heart into the latter efforts; behavior like that did not come naturally to him, and he wished he were doing something else, anything else, when he was in the company of a legislator reluctant to vote for one of his programs.

Roosevelt, meanwhile, was a back-slapper who, when defied, could suddenly turn into an arm-twister. He would bark at a recalcitrant Congressman, demand of him, even threaten, knowing the man's vulnerabilities, his legislative soft spots and the support that Theodore could provide him on the latter. Sometimes he would bring his face so close to his antagonist that their noses virtually touched and Roosevelt's breath was like a hot draft that his foe could not help but inhale. Often such behavior would work. The legislator would promise the president to vote as the administration wanted, then excuse himself so quickly it seemed as if he were running for cover.

It was, thus, a matter of style, and Roosevelt's policies could not be sold to the House and Senate with Taft's style. The one commanded respect, even from his enemies; the other seemed unsure of himself, even to friends. And, even worse from the former president's perspective, and despite Taft's insistence to the contrary, it seemed that he was trying to sell more and more of his own policies, fewer and fewer of Roosevelt's.

When Theodore finally set foot again in North America, he was amazed at how Quentin and Archie, the children he had so wanted to see, had grown. And with the growth, and their exposure to the various arts of France, had come a new sophistication. The two boys were thrilled to see their father again, but theirs were not the welcomes of little boys, jumping up and down, wanting daddy to pick them up. The same degree of joy was present, but it was expressed with hugs and verbal greetings, restraint rather than gymnastics. Nonetheless, they joined their siblings and mother in receiving the paterfamilias heartily, helping to ease his guilt over having been gone so long, over having missed such dramatic changes in the lives of people he loved so deeply.

But he tried to put thoughts like this behind him as quickly as he could. The patriarch of Sagamore Hill was back now, returned again to his domain and surrounded by as many members of his family as were available at the time. The world seemed once more to be spinning on its axis.

But not for long. Soon the house was empty, all the children, from Ted through Quentin, back at one school or another; and with Edith's encouragement, her husband turned his attention to the job offers awaiting him. The best, he reluctantly came to believe, was an undemanding position with a prestigious magazine called *Outlook,* where he would be an editor and contributing columnist. If he could not make the country's decisions, he could at least try to influence them. He could write what he wanted, when he wanted; he would have no quota, no minimum output required of him; the magazine, seeking even more prestige, wanted Roosevelt's name on the masthead more than his presence at the typewriter.

The former president knew it but took no offense. The reason he wavered on accepting the position was that he had never been a sedentary man; even as the nation's chief executive, he was forever pacing the corridors and grounds of the White House as he thought, talked, unwound. Now he was supposed to be cooped up in his tiny *Outlook* office all day, a mere sub-division of space in what was a building tiny enough to begin with. And he was supposed to be a mere employee, one of dozens at the magazine and hundreds of thousands at various firms in New York. This, he feared, would be the next thing to retirement for him and, after the joys of the safari and a period of rest, he was feeling even more . . . well, Rooseveltian than ever. Still, his options were limited; and after he finally said yes to *Outlook,* he began a close watch on the Taft administration, as proprietary about it as he had been about his own. He read what the newspapers and other journals had to say. He gathered information from old friends and colleagues who were eager to talk to him after his absence, to bring him up to date by expressing their displeasure with the current governance, and to provide Roosevelt with facts, figures, and anecdotes that they were willing to provide to no one else outside the government. Soon, although he had never previously anticipated such a step, Theodore began to write about the Taft presidency, turning out essays with which *Outlook* could not have been more pleased.

At first, Roosevelt's references to his successor were limited to a few words. He complimented him for being such a good-natured fellow, for having made so many friends on Capitol Hill. But then he declared that Taft was lacking the qualities of leadership. Only a few words, yes, but a sweeping condemnation; a president who could not lead was a president who could not achieve, whose programs would be pipe dreams, or else realities dictated by men stronger, more self-assured, and with greater vested interests than he.

Taft was the most sensitive of men, and to him Roosevelt's comments were not only unwarranted, but painful. The battle had officially begun — the ex-president back in the ring, feeling his opponent out, then throwing a jab here, an uppercut there. Taft knew from round one that he was over-matched, capable of little more than the occasional counterpunch, unable to be the aggressor. But Roosevelt was right: he *was* a good-natured fellow. And so, the present circumstances notwithstanding, they were still friends. Acquaintances, at least. Weren't they?

One of Taft's few successes so far, Roosevelt quickly learned, was the result of following in his predecessor's footsteps. Taft shared Roosevelt's passion for antitrust measures, and would eventually file even more lawsuits against industrial conglomerates than Roosevelt had. But with Carnegie money having funded his mission to Africa, and with the plutocracy having warmed to him somewhat now that he could no longer harm it, Theodore was not as zealous about the subject as he had been a few years earlier. Nor was he as pleased with Taft's zeal, leaving the president confounded about Roosevelt's attitude, which had once seemed the principal goal of his administration.

Further, Theodore was not pleased with Taft's positions on a variety of other issues, among them some fine points related to tariffs. But Roosevelt's real break with his successor came when he fired Gifford Pinchot as the chief of the United States Forest Service. Pinchot was not only a close friend of Theodore, but, like the ex-president, a lover of nature and a strong supporter of conservation measures. Under Roosevelt and Pinchot, the United States had set aside more land for national parks and forests than had been created in all the previous years of the country's existence. That Pinchot's firing, and the elimination of his post, automatically transferred more power to Interior Secretary Richard Ballinger, an ally of big-timber interests and a man Roosevelt believed to be indifferent to preserving the beauties of the landscape, made matters all the worse. It was, to the man most responsible for Taft's occupying the White House, an act of utter betrayal.

Yet Roosevelt's level of bile would rise even more. In 1911, Taft decided to sign an arbitration treaty with Great Britain, an act for which Theodore, in effect, called his successor a traitor. Taft was baffled again and, more than that, angered. Roosevelt himself had previously agreed to international arbitration in a conference he had attended at the Hague, hailing it as a step forward in international relations. Yet in the article he wrote about the treaty for *Outlook,* Roosevelt made no mention of his former stance, simply berating Taft's effort at diplomacy as a "sham."

In fact, as paraphrased by historian John Milton Cooper, Jr., the former president "dismissed the treaty . . . as a piece of devious diplomacy which, because it included questions of national honor and vital interest, was both unworkable and potentially dangerous to American security. Renewing his preachment on international duty, Roosevelt implored his countrymen to pursue 'righteousness first.' They must recall their glorious history of fighting for just causes and, rather than heed 'the timid and short-sighted apostles of ease and of slothful avoidance of duty,' they should dare to play 'the part of the just man armed.' "

Up to this point, Taft, as was his nature, had kept silent. No more. He was not ready to take on Roosevelt publicly yet, but to a friend he wrote that his one-time ally "believes in war and wishes to be a Napoleon and to die on the battle field. He has the spirit of the old berserkers." Word of the president's sentiments soon made the rounds of Washington insiders. Taft knew they would, and sadly awaited reports of his old friend's fury. There would be a hiatus before they came.

22

Nineteen-eleven, the year of the treaty, was also the year when the Roosevelts celebrated their silver wedding anniversary. Some of the family gathered for the occasion on December 2, then the whole of them assembled for a Sagamore Hill Christmas three weeks later, renewing congratulations for the twenty-five years of marriage, celebrating another of many family reunions.

The ex-president was in tolerable spirits for the occasion, observing the season in part by putting aside, as much as his grudge-holding nature would allow, his ill feelings toward Taft. But another negative feeling crept in to take its place, and an unaccustomed one for Roosevelt: a certain melancholy. It was the grandest time of the year, or was supposed to be, and had always been in the past. This year, though, with his children grown but unmarried — or, in Alice's case, married but childless — there were no little ones running around the house wildly, squealing with anticipation, tearing open gifts, arguing with one another about Santa's treatment of them and then making up and then fighting and making up again, swapping their gifts and then swapping them back. What, Theodore asked himself, was Christmas without tots? Without noise, confusion? Where was the festive in the festivities? The loneliest times are the ones that have in the past led to the most rejoicing.

One evening after dinner, the family was standing in the North Room, the largest in the house, everyone with a drink of one sort or another in hand. Roosevelt looked around at his loved ones, his eyes for the moment as lifeless as those of his animal heads. He did not speak until a lull finally came in the conversation, a lull made all the more noticeable because the patriarch made no move to fill it. It seemed that everyone was waiting for him to speak. The season, he finally said, "loses some of its fine edge when the youngest child is a boy a half inch taller than his father!" Quentin smiled, but uncertainly; like the rest of the family, he was not able to read his father's mood, or understand the reasons leading to it.

23

The political feud resumed at the first of the year, and it might have been Roosevelt's impatience for it that had made him feel so out of sorts over the holiday. By this time, the two men had become so estranged that Theodore contemplated taking the White House back from the incumbent. Before

197

long, he decided he had no choice but to try. Taft was horrified. He was not alone. Roosevelt's intention was a startling one for the country and a divisive one for his party, setting Republican against Republican and ensuring that the 1912 convention, to be held later that summer, would be a battleground like none that had ever preceded it.

But Theodore could not wait that long. He fired the first shot long before the convention began, accusing Taft of tampering with the delegate selection process to favor his own candidacy. It was true, of course; piling up delegates had long been, and continues to be, one of the unacknowledged perks of the presidency. But Taft denied it, stating on a campaign stop that "Mr. Roosevelt does not understand the rule for fair dealing." Reporters asked him to expand on the comment. Taft would not. In fact, although another ten or fifteen minutes remained before the train was scheduled to chug ahead to its next stop, he turned away from his listeners after the remark and promptly disappeared from the platform at the back of the train.

His staff was caught unaware. So were the men and women of the small midwestern community who had come to listen to him; after a few seconds of muttering, they gradually began to disperse, sharing their bafflement with one another. Where had Taft gone? Why, all of a sudden? Was he sick?

Taft had never done anything like this before, never just disappeared, virtually in mid-sentence. After a minute or two during which they were too numbed to act, aides and associates, as well as journalists traveling with the party, began looking for the president. But without luck. Not, that is, until a reporter, wandering by himself, ventured into the president's private railroad car, parked on a nearby siding, an idea that should have occurred to someone in the search party at the very start. And there he was. William Howard Taft. President of the United States. Sitting alone in utter darkness.

Had it been Roosevelt, he would have excoriated the intruding journalist, especially since he hadn't even knocked. But Taft simply looked up, as if he had been expecting a visitor. Neither man spoke for a few moments. Then the reporter asked Taft whether he was all right. Softly and sadly: "Roosevelt was my closest friend," he said, and then gave way to the tears he had been struggling to hold back.

The incident was not reported. The press did not print such tales in those days. Surely

Roosevelt never knew of it. If so, he would not have been moved. "Mr. Taft is president," he said at about this time, "only because I kept my promise in spite of infinite pressure to break it. It is a bad trait to bite the hand that feeds you." The fact that Roosevelt believed Taft, weakened by his sorrow, was instead engaged in hand-biting is an example of grudge-holding to the utmost.

When the convention finally began in Chicago that June, Roosevelt left all restraint behind. He took on Taft in a manner at once vicious and infantile: the president was "a fathead," "a puzzle-wit," a man with "brains less than those of a guinea-pig." It was a shameful performance, Roosevelt's excoriation reflecting far more poorly on himself than it did on Taft.

Who responded by calling Roosevelt "a dangerous egotist," a "demagogue," and a person who simply "could not tell the truth." It was milder language than Roosevelt's, but hostile for Taft, especially when discussing a public figure in a public forum.

The Republicans were fighting a civil war.

When the time came for the convention to vote on its presidential candidate, it validated Roosevelt's charge of delegate tampering by naming Taft as its nominee even though Roosevelt had defeated Taft by a significant margin in almost all of the party's primaries and was clearly the favorite of the GOP majority. And Taft knew it. His position could not have been a more awkward one, and he showed it with an acceptance speech timidly delivered and frequently interrupted — a few boos here, a few there, continually scattered shouts of "Roosevelt, Roosevelt, we want Roosevelt!" So many hard feelings; old-timers would long afterward say they could remember nothing like the convention of 1912.

Roosevelt harbored more of those hard feelings than anyone else. Taft might have defeated him at the convention, but it would not, he vowed in silent but unalterable rage, happen again.

Quentin, meanwhile, was hearing things that disturbed him. He was hearing that his father and President Taft were not best buddies anymore. He was also hearing about columns his father had written, for *Outlook* and various newspapers, in which he described Taft in a manner that was not only unkind but sometimes just plain nasty. Quentin did not read the papers, but word of the rift made its way to him anyhow. It was, to say the least, confusing.

He thought of asking his father about it, but decided not to. It was not his business. It was adult business, and his father might be angry at him for thinking he had any right to know the details.

Besides, what troubled the boy most was not Roosevelt's relationship with his successor; it was his own relationship with Taffy. True, Quentin did not see much of his old pal anymore, but there had always been comfort for him in knowing he could call on Taffy if he had to. Roosevelt might not have thought the White House was in good hands with Taft, but Quentin could not help thinking back to the days when the mansion's more playful activities were in the best of hands with himself and Taffy.

There was no denying, however, that the two boys were drifting apart at an ever-accelerating rate. Quentin might have been a letter writer, but Taffy was not. A telephone call was a special occasion, an odd, new form of communication with which neither boy was comfortable. And Sagamore Hill was a long way from Washington, D.C. Was the friendship eroding naturally, the inevitable way of things when children grow older and distance becomes too much of an obstacle to overcome? Or was it more personal, the result of their fathers' mutual hostility seeping down to their offspring? Quentin used to be the head of the White House Gang, Taffy his loyal assistant; now the Gang no longer existed, as the fathers of many of its members were no longer employed by the Taft administration. The bond between the two boys, it seemed, was no more, either. Even when they got back to Washington after the convention, neither made an attempt to contact the other. Quentin felt it was his responsibility to do so, but was afraid an overture from him would be unwelcome by anyone in the Taft family. Fourteen years old, he was, and already looking back at the good old days.

It was about the time when Quentin was snapping out of his gloominess that Roosevelt shocked the world of American politics once more. First there was his challenge to the incumbent for the Republican nomination. Now he announced a challenge not only to Taft but to the Democratic candidate as well, former Princeton University president and single-term New Jersey Governor Woodrow Wilson. Having been swindled out of the nomination by his own party, Roosevelt declared, he would run for president with the backing of another party. There would be three, not two, candidates for president this year. And the third would be a terror!

Even Theodore had never stirred controversy like this before. Even Theodore had never made headlines like this. Some journalists praised his courage. Others berated his heresy. All gave him far more space, at least at the beginning of the campaign, than the Republican and Democrat candidates put together.

Roosevelt's friends, in addition to thoughtful Republicans who knew him only casually, many of them members of the House or Senate, tried in every way they could to talk their one-time leader out of such a rebellious act. It would, they said, only split the Republican vote, thereby handing the presidency to Wilson on a silver platter. Roosevelt's candidacy, in other words, was an act of selfishness, if not even sabotage, and would have repercussions for the entire country. Maybe even the world. Surely he could see the inevitability of such a result; surely he would not want someone as delicate, as inexperienced, as Wilson occupying his former home. Roosevelt heard it every day, read it in every paper, knew it was the consensus of people in both parties.

But he didn't care. He refused to listen.

He had gotten up such a head of steam that he could not have stopped himself if he'd wanted to. Besides, there was a principle involved here, Roosevelt asserted, and principle must be heeded above all. In brief, two men who did not have the ability, courage, or experience to lead the United States were seeking to do just that. It was imperative, then, that another man, one of proven ability, unquestioned courage, and years of experience offer himself to the populace. That candidate, Roosevelt proclaimed, would most certainly win.

Or would he? After a time, having calmed down a bit and begun to consider the possibility that a Wilson victory really *would* be the outcome of a third-party bid, Roosevelt decided to seek counsel from those whose opinions meant most to him. Unfortunately, they were all members of his family, not a politically savvy person among them. He gathered as many of his kinfolk as were available around the dining room table at Sagamore one evening, and wrote letters to a few others. He told them of his choice: he could either listen to the truth of his inner voice and continue to fight the just battle, or listen to the naysayers and yield to expediency. He outlined the positions of the three candidates on various issues, and pointed out that his positions were in all cases the best — not only the most sensible, but the most popular among the American citizenry. Roosevelt was not so much seeking counsel from those he gathered as he was stacking the deck.

Which, as he well knew, was unnecessary. There was, among his advisers, no dissent. Theodore had always taken Edith's advice seriously; but, as he had first begun to realize at Christmas, he should also heed the counsel of his children, the six young men and women who were children no more. They might not be experienced in the world of politics, but they were all intelligent and, being Roosevelts, none was afraid to speak his mind honestly. Because of her marriage of inconvenience to Nicholas Longworth, Alice was probably more knowledgeable about the back roads of political maneuvering than any of the other siblings, and she not only supported her father's candidacy, she surprised one and all by announcing that she would actively campaign for him. Her husband, who pained her with his constant philandering, was a fellow Ohioan who had already announced his support for Taft, but she didn't care; in fact, the idea of piquing him by supporting her father was probably part of her motivation. Regardless,

Roosevelt was genuinely touched and, in thanking her, met her gaze warmly. Although she was her own woman now, twenty-eight years old and mellower than she had been in the past, she still needed a father figure. Her own father, she had apparently decided, would have to do.

Roosevelt had once boasted that he was as strong as a bull moose. As his decision to run in 1912 indicated, he certainly demonstrated the stubbornness of such a beast. It seemed, then, as good a nickname as any for the band of dissidents that he would lead to the polls. The Bull Moose Party, as the press referred to it, although it was officially known as the Progressive Party, was dedicated, according to its mission statement, "to dissolve the unholy alliance between corrupt business and corrupt politics." It was a perfect summary of Roosevelt's political philosophy.

In the wake of his nomination for the presidency that summer, life at home took a decided turn for the frantic. Edith was appalled, as unable to face the prospect of such a bitter campaign as she would have been to face another safari; and the more crowded the house became with her husband's fellow Bull Moosers, strategizing and scheming, the more desperately she sought peace in unused rooms, private nooks. However,

> Quentin was still boy enough to enjoy the political activity at Sagamore Hill (daily delegations, a constant racket of typewriters and telegraphers, reporters camping out on the lawn) without any curiosity about what, exactly, was going on. In an affectionate pen portrait written that summer, his father described him as "tranquil, efficient, moon-faced and entirely merry. . . ."

But, fortunately for Edith, the candidate spent little time during the campaign at home. In his quest for a return to the nation's highest office, Roosevelt proved a tireless traveler, more so than either Taft or Wilson. He orated more than his foes, wrote more newspaper and magazine articles than his foes, covered more ground than they. And so it was that on a gray, chilly October afternoon three weeks before the election, he found himself in Milwaukee, Wisconsin, being driven down the main street in a roofless car despite the weather. His destination was the city's main auditorium, where he would make yet another speech.

Hundreds upon hundreds of people lined the sidewalks, in some places half a dozen or more deep. Their response to Roosevelt was overwhelming, more than he had expected, perhaps more than he had received at any other stop in the campaign. When the cheers reached a crescendo, he ordered the driver of his car to stop. Roosevelt stood, his teeth gleaming despite the day's bleakness, his arms waving from side to side, energetically grateful. He nodded, tossing out both thank-yous and campaign slogans to the crowd.

What he did not do, unfortunately, was duck.

A bartender named John Schrank, who had once dreamed of assassinating President McKinley, had come to the belief that "any man looking for a third term ought to be shot," and had made up his mind that he was the man for the job. Schrank had had a dream not long before, he would later claim, in which McKinley had spoken to him, pointing to Roosevelt and hissing, "This is my murderer; avenge my death." All the more reason for him to act.

He had bought a revolver in New York a few weeks earlier and followed Roosevelt halfway across the country, waiting for the precise moment, the precise angle. And here

209

it was. Schrank had dissolved into the crowd in Milwaukee and, finding his target but a few feet from him, virtually taunting him with his visibility, he aimed the revolver and fired a single shot. It struck Roosevelt in the chest. Theodore dropped into a sitting position on the back seat, and his head leaned to the side as if it had come loose from his neck. The driver could hear him groan.

Schrank was immediately grabbed by the people around him, who flung him to the ground and subdued him with punches, kicks, and improvised wrestling holds. A stenographer who had accompanied Roosevelt was, it seemed, trying to break Schrank's neck. However, like McKinley before him, Roosevelt tried to call off the mayhem.

"Stand back! Don't hurt that man!" he is reported to have said, albeit weakly. And then he asked for the man to be brought to him.

Several of Roosevelt's admirers dragged Schrank in front of the candidate, who was still slumped on the seat, barely moving, his breath coming in spurts, each an extraordinary effort.

Schrank was described, although not by his victim, as a "dull-eyed man," possessing the "unmistakable expressionlessness of insanity, along with clothes that looked as though they had been slept in for weeks, and an enormous pair of shoes." Theodore mustered the energy to lift his head and looked at his assailant for a few seconds. "What did you do it for?" He got no response. "Oh, what's the use," he groaned. "Turn him over to the police."

As he was being hustled into custody, people nearby crowded around Roosevelt, looking down at him, especially at his shirt. The front of it was red, deep red, a spreading, bloody mess, and they were horrified. Roosevelt, however, was not. Having coughed and not brought up any blood, he had determined that his wound was not serious. And how could it be? He had been as lucky as the target of a deranged gunman could possibly have been, even able to smile as he patted the inside pocket of his suit coat.

In the pocket was a thick sheaf of papers, a copy of his speech; also, a steel case for his eyeglasses. The bullet had struck him in precisely this spot — and so, he deduced, it was impossible for a missile to have had enough momentum to penetrate his chest wall and reach the lung. He was right. It did not. So he was in pain, but not danger.

Pain he could endure. Pain would not stop him.

Digging into his pocket, he pulled out the speech — fifty pages that were actually twice that thickness because they had been folded over. In almost the exact middle was a ragged hole. He showed it to the people surrounding him, so many now having gathered. "There is a bullet — there is where the bullet went through — and it probably saved me from it going into my heart." Roosevelt also held up the eyeglasses case, showing it to the crowd. He was gaining strength, of will if not of body. "The bullet is in me now, so that I cannot make a very long speech but I will try my best. . . ."

Which would, given the Roosevelt resolve, probably be good enough.

To his traveling companions, though, the notion was lunacy. A man gets shot in the heart — although, granted, a heavily protected heart — and then intends to give a speech? His staff pleaded with him not to do it, to go to the hospital, not the auditorium. So did the Wisconsin Republicans and Progressives who had scheduled the event. Even the man behind the wheel of the candidate's car supported the consensus. At least, all agreed, let them summon a doctor.

Roosevelt would have none of it. He buttoned his jacket to cover the spreading bloodstain and tugged himself to more of an upright position in the seat. Let's keep going, he ordered, seeming now in control of his breath. His driver shook his head but did as he was told. The members of his staff had no choice but to follow along, some still pleading with the candidate in his wake.

Reaching the Milwaukee Auditorium, Roosevelt entered through a back door and told the man who would introduce him to get started right away and keep it short. He, too, did as commanded. Whereupon Roosevelt pushed aside a curtain, after similarly pushing away a number of people blocking his path as they kept urging to summon an ambulance, threatening to do it for him, refusing to allow this act of masochism. Roosevelt turned on them, demanding their acquiescence. He had agreed to make a speech; he would make it. Those who cared about his health had no choice but to give way to his determination.

The speaker took the stage. He was greeted with a roaring ovation. He did not want it; it took too much time. Signaling the audience to stop, he asked them "to be as quiet as possible. I don't know whether you fully understand that I have just been shot, but it takes more than that to kill a

213

bull moose."

The thousands of people gathered before him, not knowing what had happened, were mystified by the statement, unsure they had heard him correctly. A few gasped. Everyone turned to someone else for clarification, which was impossible. The whole of them created a murmur that ran through the auditorium like the hum of a small machine. But it quickly died out; Roosevelt wanted stillness, and he got it.

He proceeded to talk for the full hour and a half that his words required, perhaps longer, as he lacked his usual fire. At least, having delivered the address many times before, he knew it well enough that he did not have to struggle to read the words that had been obliterated by the bullet hole.

But, in every other way, Roosevelt *did* struggle. Constantly weakening, he held on to the sides of the podium, ever more tightly, eventually white-knuckled. He leaned his chest into it; surely he would have fallen without its support. His skin was pale and the pallor increased as the minutes went by, beads of perspiration dripping down his forehead, soaking his collar. Sometimes his voice sank to a whisper. He might have been fortunate that the bullet had struck him where it did, but if he lost enough blood, he would be just as fatally wounded as if the folded-over speech and steel case had been in a different pocket.

Some people in the audience did some gripping of their own — reflexively hanging on to their armrests, also white-knuckled, as they watched him — hoping, in their confusion, that Roosevelt could go on while at the same time they wished he were not making the effort. It was a night of high drama.

At some point during the speech, Edith, who was at the theatre in New York watching a performance of Johann Strauss's *The Merry Countess,* got the news of her husband. She broke into tears and ran for the closest door. "Take me to where I can talk to him or hear from him at once," she demanded of her entourage. The Progressive Party's National Headquarters were located nearby, in a Manhattan hotel, and a police escort sped her there as soon as she entered the car. The headquarters had an open phone line to Milwaukee.

As for the children, they did not learn of the shooting until the next day, after they had had their night's rest and their father was out of danger. Still, scattered at their various schools, they were chilled by the knowledge that Theodore had come so close to meeting his predecessor's fate, and for the first time began to wonder whether, at some point in the future, it would actually happen. They could be excused for wondering why the President of the United States seemed as much a target as an object of veneration.

Roosevelt's subject that night, as it had been on so many other nights in so many other cities, was the need for the Progressive Movement in American politics. He was devoted to it, he said, "with my whole heart and soul." It was one of several occasions during the speech when he was interrupted by applause. When he finished, the entire assemblage stood as one and roared their approval. And relief. It is doubtful that they were able to pay as much attention to Roosevelt's words as they had intended, but their admiration for his courage was boundless.

The candidate acknowledged the gratitude as long as he could, and then, emptied of the adrenaline, collapsed into the arms of his companions that had been propelling him and finally allowed himself to be taken to a hospital. But not until he endured yet more agony, this of the "friendly fire" type. So many people in the audience so deeply appreciated Roosevelt's show of courage that night that they rushed the stage and, incredibly, according to Edmund Morris, some of them "crowded around and tried to slap his back. Charles Thompson [a *New York Times* reporter] got the distinct impression that each man was intent on being the last to shake hands with Theodore Roosevelt. They were pushed away, and [Roosevelt], walking very slowly, was led back to his car."

At the Milwaukee Emergency Hospital, Theodore's own diagnosis was confirmed — wound minor, but blood loss great. He needed rest and a lack of stimulation, especially after having tortured himself by such lengthy speechifying; doctors insisted that he stay the night, maybe longer. Roosevelt insisted otherwise. Unfortunately, there was no medical school in the country that prepared its students to defy a man with the temperament of a bull moose.

After the wound was cleaned and the bleeding stopped, an antiseptic was applied and a nurse carefully bandaged the affected area. Then Roosevelt pretended to listen to instructions for further care of himself and to a lecture on the foolishness of his departure. He slipped on his bloody shirt, the blood having now dried and hardened like a piece of cardboard, and thanked the hospital staff profusely. He smiled at them and waved over his shoulder, departing as casually as if the emergency room had been on his schedule all along, right after the auditorium, just another day on the campaign trail.

The 1912 election went exactly as predicted, or, as a Republican would have put it, exactly as feared. Roosevelt got more votes than Taft that autumn, but the two of them divided the Republican total and Woodrow Wilson, whom many regarded as more of an academic than a chief executive, became the unlikely president of the United States.

Taft, also a scholar more than a chief executive, accepted a position teaching law at Yale and went on, to his abiding satisfaction, to become the Chief Justice of the United States Supreme Court. His placid and thoughtful manner suited him perfectly for positions both on the faculty and on the bench. He did not hold on to his resentment against Roosevelt; he was not that kind of man. He was, rather, saddened and bewildered that the two of them, once so close, had ended up unspeaking adversaries. There was no longer any contact between them.

Roosevelt, on the other hand, does not

seem to have given their splintered relationship much thought, and when he did he blamed Taft for not stepping aside so that Roosevelt could have prevented Wilson's assumption of the presidency. Theodore also blamed Wilson, just on general principles, inbred dislike. Did he blame himself for either the personal or electoral outcomes? It seems not. "There is no repentance in my soul," he wrote to a friend, after he had had time to think things over, "and I am not the least responsible for the present conditions."

24

Roosevelt had needed to get away after surrendering the nation's highest office in 1909. He found himself with the same desire after losing it one presidential term later. He had to escape from Republicans who were irate at him. He had to escape from Progressives, who wanted to build a larger, more influential party around him, one that could take the White House in 1916. And, as had been the case previously, he had to escape from reporters, whose numbingly inane questions were like a form of water torture to him. Once again, Roosevelt found himself thinking of destinations.

His first was domestic. He took Quentin,

Archie, and Nicholas, Theodore's first cousin once removed, via train to the Southwest. "The trip," Nicholas later wrote, "combined sightseeing (the Grand Canyon, the Painted Desert, Hopi villages) with hunting (most notably cougars in northern Arizona)." The boys would be thrilled with both the scenery and the company. Not to mention the cougars.

It was a long trip, several days and nights on the train. But the farther west they got, the more colorful and rugged were the landscapes that slid by their windows all day, terrain like nothing they had ever seen in the East. And, more important to Quentin and Archie, they had their father all to themselves for almost a week. It was the longest they had enjoyed such companionship in their lives. Their father had no trouble treating the boys like the young men they were becoming; his sons, on the other hand, treated their father like a possession of inestimable value, one that, at least for the time being, was theirs and theirs alone.

For Quentin, the journey's first memorable moment came when he rode around the rim of the Grand Canyon on muleback with Theodore, just the two of them, admiring nature's grandeur. A second was a ceremony the visitors witnessed a few days later in which cigar-smoking Hopi Indian priests not only washed rattlesnakes, but "kept them at bay by stroking them with feather wands. [Roosevelt] was intrigued by the sinuous movements of both man and reptile. They seemed to share a temporary accord in which, however, the threat of sudden violence lurked." The Hopis obviously had a reason for all this, but it eluded the Roosevelt party entirely. It was, nonetheless, a grand show.

Finally, as recounted by Nicholas, there appeared a sight like no other on their journey. "Rounding a little projection in the [Rainbow Natural Bridge Canyon]," he wrote, "we saw before us an enormous red sandstone arch shaped like a rainbow, stretching from one side of the canyon across to the other. It was difficult to grasp the enormous size of it until we came beneath it. Then TR, Archie, Quentin and I lay down on our backs and looked up at it as the sun was going behind the cliff walls. In this manner we could see the enormous beam of the arch, as high above us as the vault of a cathedral."

More memorable moments, although of a quite different kind, were just ahead.

When the foursome left their train so that

Roosevelt could hike through some pathless hills to search for his cougars, Quentin and Archie were ordered to lag behind. They did not need to be told. They had never seen their father hunt before and, further, had never seen a beast as powerful as a cougar in the wild. When they got their first look at one, even from afar, they began to lag even more.

Roosevelt chuckled. What man can resist the chance to show off for his sons.

His rifle loaded, the cougar in the midst of his crosshairs, Roosevelt steadied himself for a few seconds and squeezed the trigger. A shot, maybe two or three, later, the animal was dead. To Quentin it seemed a remarkable feat, and even though he had long known his father was capable of it, actually seeing him bring down so powerful an animal left the boy speechless. It was one thing to be the son of a president; quite another to be the son of a big-game hunter. His three slain rabbits, about which he had not thought for a long time, now seemed less an accomplishment than ever.

But a few cougars in the Southwest were not enough to satisfy Roosevelt's quest for adventure, nor to raise his flagging spirits in the wake of electoral defeat. After returning to Sagamore Hill for a brief respite, he once more disappointed his family by taking off for distant lands. This time it was the uncharted wilds of Brazil and the perilous jungles surrounding the Amazon River. As was the case with the safari, Kermit would be his first mate. Unlike the safari, the physical punishment that lay ahead would be almost fatal for a fifty-five-year-old man and, to one degree or another, would linger with him for the rest of his days.

The venture was not Roosevelt's doing. It had long been the passion of Cândido Rondon, a Brazilian military officer and explorer, and its purpose was geographic. Of course, the former American president, Rondon, and their fellow explorers would kill a number of animals along the way, sending several of them back to the United States — but it would be nothing to compare with the totals Roosevelt and company had amassed in Africa.

Instead, he and Rondon devoted most of their attention to another goal, finding the headwaters of the Rio da Dúvida, the River of Doubt, and tracing it to its source, the Amazon. It had never been done before, and the explorers were quick to discover why: the going could not have been more difficult or more dangerous, nor the setting more otherworldly. "The skies were the home of bloodsucking vampire bats," according to Roosevelt biographer H. W. Brands, "which siphoned the very life liquid out of mammals of the four- and two-legged varieties. A person seeking relief from the insects or the bats might take refuge in the nearest stream; if so, he wouldn't last long if that stream were home, as it likely was, to piranhas, the flesh-eating fish that could strip every ounce of soft tissue from the body of a horse or man within minutes, leaving only bare bones awash in blood water."

When Roosevelt wrote his own article on the trip for *Outlook,* he colored it with "almost gothic grotesqueness." It was not, as some suspected, a fictional touch.

As for the Rio da Dúvida itself, it was as wide as a city block in some places, as narrow as Kermit's rifle was long — he actually measured — in others; it was as calm as a puddle in some places, its rapids tumultuous and overwhelming elsewhere. When the river or rapids became impassable, the men had to portage, and the jungle through which they proceeded was not meant for human transit, so thick was it with trees and grasses, with vegetation they could not identify, and with gnarled undergrowth that sheltered who-knew-what kinds of sneaky, lethal animal life.

For all these reasons, the party proceeded slowly, more slowly than they had expected at the start; their provisions, thus, had to be rationed, and eventually hunger became the greatest obstacle of all. Roosevelt and his companions began to dream of food, to talk about it, as sailors long at sea might talk about the delights of a woman. According to George Cherrie, an ornithologist on the trek, "Colonel Roosevelt always wanted a mutton chop 'with a tail to it!' " As for Kermit, he favored "a bowl of strawberries and cream."

Nothing of the sort was available. There is reason to believe, though, by this point in his life, that Kermit had brought a few bottles of liquor with him, stashed away for an emergency.

It is doubtful that his father knew he was resorting to alcohol, doubtful even that Theodore could pay much attention to his boy. Roosevelt was growing sicker by the day, and consequently less perceptive about both his companions and his surroundings. As the ex-president faded, Kermit became more and more important to him, although the journey was such a struggle that it sapped the younger man's strength as well.

But the two of them did what they could to provide mutual encouragement, swearing to each other to persevere, and sustaining each other with their large store of family memories. There had probably never been a time when the father so needed one of his children, and even so, family memories were becoming more and more of a blur as the days slogged on.

At about the same time, Quentin was preparing for an adventure of his own, although much more modest than his father's. The sixteen-year-old would return to Arizona, which had become almost a fantasyland to him since his previous visit. But this time he would travel without his family, leaving all supervision behind. Edith, long since used to her menfolk's definition of manhood, did not try to dissuade him.

But, in fact, it did not seem as if he would face any hardships. Quentin had signed up for a packhorse tour that would cover some of the same terrain he had seen before, as well as some new, but no more menacing, vistas. The pace would be leisurely, the skies blue and sunny. The men leading the way were experienced hands at this kind of thing; freak accidents just did not happen.

Except to Quentin. "A packhorse had

slipped and rolled over on him," reported one of his father's biographers, "dislodging two ribs where they joined the spine. It was not the kind of trauma a youth needed just when he was testing the limits of his new adult body." He had also wrenched his back, and the latter injury would never completely heal.

Quentin pleaded with his mates not to let his mother know, and in fact there was no convenient way for them to do so even if they had wanted. After a few days, the lad's injuries were troubling him less and there seemed no reason to alarm anyone at home.

Despite the ever-threatening terrain, the Rondon-Roosevelt pilgrimage would eventually achieve its goal, the men becoming the first ever to locate the upper tributaries of the Rio da Dúvida. Their success would later be commemorated by the Brazilian government in a number of ways, one of which was that, henceforth, the River of Doubt was no longer to be known by its previous name, but as the Rio Roosevelt, or, to some, the Rio Teodoro.

The former American president, recently humbled by his nation's electorate, was humbled in a different way by such an honor. The Nobel Peace Prize was one thing, but to have his name attached to the map, where it would reside evermore in a land never to be tamed, was quite another.

Unfortunately, he was humbled yet again by the parlous state of his health. While sailing down the eponymous river of the future, Roosevelt had suffered a recurrence of the malaria he had contracted in Cuba, as well as an infection from a leg wound, incurred earlier on his South American adventure, that had not been properly treated. And that, in turn, reactivated his more serious leg injury from the carriage accident a decade ago. Eventually, his leg became seriously inflamed, a curse known as erysipelas, which, among other things, would often spread over other parts of the body, both skin and mucous membranes.

The one-time Rough Rider was weaker than he had ever been as a child, racked by disease, injury, and malnutrition. Cherrie, who was himself fighting dysentery, looked at Roosevelt one evening, with a thick purple darkness falling around the campsite, and said, "I don't believe he can live through the night."

He did, of course, but there were other nights when the odds seemed even less in his favor. On one of them, his fever reaching 103, his chest aching so much that he could barely breathe, and his consciousness giving way to frequent hallucinations, Roosevelt asked Rondon to leave him behind, just stretch him out to die under one of the towering palms on the Amazon's banks. He did not, he said, want to be a burden to others.

Rondon would not even think of deserting so prominent a man, a man who had been such an unyielding force his entire life. Neither would Kermit, who, a week or so previously, had almost drowned on the journey. Neither would Jose Cajazeira, the expedition's doctor, who was certain his patient's health and spirits would improve. And neither would anyone else accompanying the great American through this South American heart of darkness. Theodore had no choice, then, but to yield to their overwhelming respect for him and, in time, with Rondon and Kermit looking after him, alternating every twelve hours; with Kermit almost surely turning to whiskey to fortify himself for the long shifts; and with Dr. Cajazeira providing medications and advice, Roosevelt did in fact regain his health. But not all of it, and not all the time. He was able to finish the journey, but did so, it seemed, with little time remaining before the journey finished him.

As a result, when he got back to the United States in 1913, Theodore Roosevelt looked a mockery of himself. His appearance startled his wife and children. Quentin's initial reaction, although he did his best not to let it show, was a combination of fright and sympathy. His father had lost so much weight that his clothes hung on his body as if on wire hangers, and his cheeks had hollowed, gathering wrinkles. He was worn, fragile, suddenly old, listlessness having replaced his usual vigor. His voice had suddenly become that of an older man as well. He told one of his friends that going to South America had taken ten years off his life, and he might have been right. Then again, the arithmetic be damned! — he still believed, as he always had, he would die when he reached sixty.

Roosevelt was not too ill, however, to be fretful, and nothing ate at him more than the fact that, at his age, he did not believe he could "make his body" again. There was not enough time left to him, and he no longer possessed either the ability or the will. He had gone to war against both Spaniards and the wildlife of Africa and won on both occasions. But when he challenged the River of Doubt, the river won by attrition. It was, he could not help thinking, the one challenge of his life he should not have accepted.

25

Once again, Roosevelt had returned to Sagamore Hill after an adventure, but this time familiar surroundings did not re-energize him for further deeds. Ethel moved in for a few days to assist Edith with her father's care, but despite her ministrations and the constant letters and visits from his family; despite the daisies in full bloom and the damp breezes off Long Island Sound fluttering the leaves of the maples and oaks and the single copper beech; despite sunny days and comfortable moonlit nights, a pall had settled over Theodore, a feeling he had never known before. He might be home again, but he had also entered the wilderness again, although a different kind than he had previously encountered, one for which his typically aggressive nature would be a liability, not an asset.

For this was a wilderness of inactivity and political treacheries, a wilderness with its own kind of threatening terrain, its own kind of beasts ready to pounce, hiding alongside trails that seemed to lead nowhere, rather than to the kind of prestige that had once been Roosevelt's uniquely. It was not just the Republicans and Progressives who continued to make life difficult for him with their pleas for his candidacy; Theodore also found himself more and more troubled by Democrats who continually ignored him or scorned him themselves for their own reasons. Wilson's presidency was, after all, a repudiation of almost everything that Roosevelt had stood for, and Wilson's first term was thought by a majority to be successful. This wilderness, to Theodore, was one of defiance and heartache.

But gradually his attitude began to change. He regained some of his appetite and put a few pounds back on. He began to talk more expressively, resonantly. He seemed to capture a spark, a sharpness in his eyes. Yet he still found himself a different man, less voluble than his younger self. He did not go so far as to indulge in self-pity — he would never do such a thing — but he was baffled that the gods would allow such treatment of a man of his stature.

Unable to find a way out of his new wilderness, Roosevelt was forced to carve out a clearing and survive within it. He gave speeches that lacked their characteristic fire and eloquence; wrote books that sold well but did not influence policy or restore his prestige; denounced Wilson in both the speeches and the books; and even pursued jaguars and wild boars on a brief sojourn back to South America, one which he undertook against all advice and common sense, simply to prove to himself that he could do it. He could, but it was an effort, and he would not discuss how comfortable his companions had made the hunt for him, how solicitous had been their treatment. Perhaps on occasion they had even steadied the rifle for him. He must have realized it was the last time he would ever take on big game, but so be it. Some time had to be the last. For a period that was all too brief, he was happy enough to be back in the hunt without feeling he would not survive it.

Best of all, in this new phase of his life, Roosevelt welcomed grandchildren into the world, thanks initially to Ted. He calculated that, before he turned sixty, one or two of them would be old enough to run through the house at Christmas, restoring some of the old warmth to the holiday.

He also did his best to keep up with Quentin, who had turned into "an affection-ate, soft hearted, overgrown puppy kind of boy." But, although soon to graduate, he had never managed to adjust to Groton, and there were times when he seemed uncharacteristically morose.

His performance in the classroom was, for the most part, well above average. Despite occasional fevers, now-and-then headaches, part-time pain in his sinuses that sometimes shot through his entire body, and the occasional backaches from the packhorse accident, he was more often than not able to display his usual vigor and enthusiasm, and was almost always near the top of his class. His father had not expected it. "Heavens!" he wrote to Quentin. "To think of one of our family standing as high as that! It's almost paralyzing."

But Quentin's behavior out of the classroom was not as exemplary. He had kept his promise to refrain from public nudity, but defied curfews, ran through hallways in which walking was the prescribed pace, and shouted in settings that demanded quieter speech. He was also known to express his opinion of faculty or administrators or other adults who struck him as unpardonably stuffy by wearing a lampshade on his head in their presence.

No one, in Quentin's view, was more worthy of his donning a lampshade, or more generally unacceptable, than Endicott Peabody, not only Groton's headmaster but its founder. To others in his field, the man was a hero. When Yale presented him with an honorary degree, it did so with an encomium effusive to the point of embarrassment.

> What strength is to weakness, what experience is to ignorance or blind confidence, what light and faith are to darkness and doubt, what courage is to trembling fear, what the spiritual potter is to the pliant clay of youthful character, what Paul was to Timothy — that, all that, is the Head Master of Groton School to the young manhood blessed with his devoted instruction and companionship.

Had he heard the above, Quentin would have pushed the lampshade down around his head, ever tighter. He found nothing devoted about Peabody's instruction, nothing desirable about his companionship. The "never-to-be-sufficiently-anathematized" educator, as the youngest Roosevelt thought of him, was strict, quick to anger, and quick to punish; further, Quentin decided, he was also guilty of poor taste in literature.

One day, outside the classroom, Peabody found the boy leaning against a tree reading Bram Stoker's *Dracula*. He ordered Quentin to hand it over. Quentin refused. It was his own time, his own book; he could choose to indulge in whatever author he pleased. Yes, Peabody told him, but not material like *Dracula;* it was "not fine reading." Quentin had no choice but to surrender the volume.

But he was livid. He had been censored. In the days that followed, he pleaded with Peabody for the return of Stoker's volume, which chilled him to sleep at night and kept him awake through the more tedious classes of the day, of which, he continued to believe, there were far too many for a school of Groton's reputation. One day he made an appointment with the headmaster, dressed in his finest, and promised Peabody he would reform. No more pranks, no more disobedience. He would be an example to others at the school, a source of constant pride to his family, his nation, the world. All Peabody had to do was return the book, which wasn't school property to begin with!

The headmaster would have none of it. He had heard it all before from young Roosevelt and was wise not to believe it. That Peabody had behaved improperly in confiscating the personal property of a student did not concern him; Groton was *his* school; he would do as he pleased, and that included prohibiting Quentin from making further entreaties. The miscreant was dismissed from the school's office and told he was not to return for any reason less than an emergency.

Quentin had never before encountered a person like this.

Upset though he was, he was at the same time bemused. The headmaster "disapproved of me strenuously," he proudly wrote to sister Alice, the most likely of all his siblings to understand his behavior. She went further, not only understanding but letting him know she fully supported him.

Relations between Quentin and Peabody grew even more contentious. Although the younger Roosevelt continued to master most of his studies during most terms, he would occasionally falter, and Peabody was quick, too quick in the boy's opinion, to attach a note to the bottom of these report cards, pointing out his failings. As early as October 23, 1909, after Quentin had been a student for but a month, Peabody wrote to his parents, "There are far too many black marks. He is, however, getting an idea of what is expected of him & I hope that next month will see a much better report." And as late as February 6, 1915: "Only fair. He could be an 85 boy if he wanted to be." But he *was* an 85 boy, almost all the time, a fact that Peabody could not bring himself to acknowledge.

Quentin was upset by the criticism, sometimes even depressed, and wondered at times whether it would turn out to be a prophecy. "I'm awfully afraid I'm going to get a bum mark this month," he wrote to his mother in 1912. "Somehow marks don't seem to go right, no matter how much I work."

But they did. In 1910, his second year at Groton, he made the honor roll, cabling the news to his mother. On his next report card, with grades even higher, was a note from Sherrard Billings, who was for a brief time the acting headmaster of Groton. "Excellent indeed. I am very pleased, as everybody is. There is no reason why he cannot keep up this record."

Peabody never wrote such a note. Quentin's grades were such that he could have written several. It remains to this day a mystery why the lord and master of the school, who had taken so well to the first three Roosevelt boys entering his domain, simply could not abide the fourth. Perhaps he had been exposed to one Roosevelt too many. Perhaps he had become annoyed with Theodore's certainty that his children were entitled to admission simply because they *were* his children. Neither is an excuse for the angst he caused a boy who did not often show his sensitive side but nonetheless felt it deeply within.

Although aware of his son's misfortunes, Roosevelt found himself too dispirited to deal with them, unwilling to contact Peabody or Billings or any of his son's teachers and plead his case. In fact, he seemed unable to admit to himself that Quentin was having difficulties in the first place; he was, after all, attending the same prep school his brothers had attended without the slightest difficulty. The most he could do was write to his youngest, whom he now considered his "literary correspondent," ignoring the boy's complaints, and blindly encouraging him. "I am very glad . . . that you are playing center on the second eleven," he said, apropos of a minor matter in his son's life. "[T]o play center on the second eleven is, I think, a pretty creditable thing. Now remember two fond and eager parents have great hopes of a prefectship next year!"

As usual, Roosevelt dictated the letter to a secretary for typing, in this case his secretary at *Outlook,* to which he had returned a few days a week when he was up to it. But as he read over his words, he decided he had not said enough. He added a few lines in his own hand. "You are all right fundamentally," he insisted; "all you have to do is keep out of mere mischief. . . ." And then the usual signature when he was writing to his children: "Your loving father, Theodore Roosevelt."

The letter, so obviously tepid, unlike anything Quentin had expected from his once-fiery father who now at times seemed doddering, had no effect on its recipient. The young man simply could not keep out of mischief. He would never settle down at Groton, never conduct himself in the manner appropriate to a Roosevelt. But his insurrection was more than just the result of his disdain for Peabody. There was also his lingering homesickness. He had been discharged from Sagamore Hill for the first time in his life when Groton beckoned, and Sagamore was his home, was what he knew, where he belonged. Even after several years, Quentin just could not adjust to its absence — and that is a long time to be homesick. He knew that his other siblings had also gone away to pursue an education. He knew it was common practice in families of the Roosevelts' social standing to pack off children to one sort of school or another. He knew it was the preparation he needed for a successful future.

But no matter. There were times when Quentin could not help but feel discarded, especially after Theodore's return from his second South American sojourn. Now both of his parents had settled in to loving and easy days at Sagamore, the place that was his last link to the life he had known in the best, most innocent of times. Emotionally, he was just not ready for the separation that would come with such inexplicable ease a short time later. Perhaps there was also a trace of guilt in knowing that, as the youngest child, his departure for Groton meant that his parents were alone. They might have been content in each other's company, but Quentin knew that his father longed for the presence of at least some of his children. However, they were absent in more ways than one, having not just gone away to school, but having outgrown pillow fighting, hide-and-seek, tag, Daddy-playing-bear-in-the-woods. All now were memories. None would ever again be activities.

It was at Groton, for reasons of which no one can be sure, that Quentin first began to show something unusual in himself, something no one had either known or foreseen earlier, something that frightened him and would certainly frighten other members of the family; he did not, therefore, discuss it with anyone, kin or friend. It was, perhaps, the result of raging hormones. Or concern about his father's health. Or his being away from home for the first time. Or a strain of the depression that had so tormented his uncle Elliott. Or, most likely, some combination of the preceding, and perhaps other factors never to be known.

But it seems that Quentin was not just a wit, not just a rebel, not just a brilliant student who did not always work up to his potential; like older brother Kermit, he too seems to have been the victim of demons. Or perhaps just a single demon. Where did it come from? Why now? Was the boy, in fact, as Theodore had insisted, "all right fundamentally"? Quenty-quee, of all people!

Then again, is "demon" the proper word at all?

When I went to sleep at night
In my little bed
I dreamed I saw a goblin
Standing near my head.

It might not have been a dream. There might really have been a goblin at Quentin's head, one that had lain dormant until prep school. Goblin is, after all, a less ominous term than demon, connoting a less fearsome creature, and is thus more in keeping with the Quentin who had given to his family such joy and comic interludes over the years. "Goblin" is also a less precise word than demon, and so can be anything from a malicious sprite to a chemical imbalance in the brain, the effects of which alter from time to time. It is a word that serves the lack of specific knowledge about Quentin's occasional woes as well as any other. Perhaps Theodore, in creating the poem, somehow sensed the eventual coming of the creature. Such a bond, after all, did the father have with his son.

The goblin first revealed itself in his writing assignments, when Quentin "tended to churn out macabre tales," in the words of family biographer Edward J. Renehan, Jr., "madness, desperation, and suicide that he did not dare show his parents. Every authority figure in Quentin's stories was a disguised version of Jack London's dark superman from *The Sea Wolf,* Wolf Larsen. And every hero was a tragic, thoughtful, existential intellectual: brave but doomed, and usually alone not just in a practical sense but a cosmic sense as well."

Unfortunately, none of Quentin's papers

from Groton still exists. No one knows precisely how he described madness and desperation; no one can say whether suicide was something only the characters contemplated, or whether it was on the author's mind as well. And in none of his letters home did Quentin ever admit how deeply he was affected by the assassination attempt on Theodore, or by his experiences on the River of Doubt, and the changes that might have come over his son as a result. It is surprising that Quentin kept his reactions to such ordeals to himself, ordeals inflicted on his beloved father. But it was the Roosevelt way. We are left to speculate on whether either of these incidents had anything to do with the goblin's taking up residence in his son's mind. The timing, if nothing else, suggests the possibility.

Then again, it might be that the goblin had given a hint of its existence long before Quentin's stay at Groton. Perhaps, if one knew how to look, it was present in circumstances that his father explained to Kermit in a 1905 letter written about the time that Theodore composed his bedtime quatrain in his son's voice. Kermit was in Oyster Bay on the occasion, Quentin in Washington. "The other day," Roosevelt wrote from the White House, "we were discussing a really dreadful accident which had happened; a Georgetown young man having taken out a young girl in a canoe on the river, the canoe upset and the girl was drowned; whereupon the young man, when he got home, took what seemed to us an exceedingly cold-blooded method of a special delivery letter to notify her parents. We were expressing our horror at his sending a special delivery letter, and Quentin solemnly chimed in with 'Yes, he wasted ten cents.' There was a moment's eloquent silence, and then we strove to explain to Quentin that what we were objecting to was not in the least the young man's spendthrift attitude."

If there truly was a goblin consorting with the youngest Roosevelt, he might well have been responsible for the boy's heartless response to the death of the young lady. If it really *was* heartless. Perhaps it was instead just a failure on the part of a boy who was only eight years old at the time to comprehend the coldness of the beau's behavior. Or, if not that, it might have been what we now call a defense mechanism, albeit a crude one, against life's harsher realities, which he had already begun to dread.

But there is another consideration as well. If a goblin *had* accompanied Quentin to sleep for a number of years, might it not have been brought into being by his brothers? However unintentionally, their actions made Quentin's childhood years more trying than they would otherwise have been. It was not just that he was the youngest of the Roosevelt males; he was also Daddy's favorite, and that meant he was automatically *not* his siblings' favorite.

This being so, it might have been that the goblin's initial role was a salutary one, that of an invisible friend, trying to help him cope with the inadvertent cruelty of kin.

Take, for instance, the time when Quentin "almost drowned after being dared by his older brothers to jump from a high rock into a deep-water cove near Oyster Bay. The brothers were constantly challenging him, the youngest, to brave each and every rite of passage they had braved. They sensed that, as the baby, he had it somewhat easier than they; they sensed he was a bit more pampered — if indeed any Roosevelt was ever pampered. Thus the others were always on him to jump long, ride fast, run far, dive deep. They pushed him again and again; and again and again he responded with good-natured perseverance.

"No Roosevelt boy ever had so many Roosevelt men to come up to the mark for."

There is no reason to go on. It is enough

to say that whatever had been building up in him before was not apparent. The story of Quentin Roosevelt did not take a visible change until some point during his Groton years, after which there was no turning back. For another side of the boy revealed itself then, a side of which so few traces are part of the historical record. Yet it is a side that would reveal itself again, more than once, and in the most disturbing form imaginable, at the most crucial time in the life of a boy who did not seem to have noticed his entrance into manhood.

THREE:
THE SOUL OF THE STORY

1

And then it happened. It finally happened. Theodore Roosevelt got his war. And not just a single day's climb up a hill in Cuba — no, nothing as simple and ephemeral and unthreatening as that. This was a *real* war, the Great War, later to be known as World War I. And maybe, just maybe, he dared to think, it was not too late for him.

On June 28, 1914, the fifty-year-old Austrian Archduke Franz Ferdinand was shot to death in Bosnia, lighting a fuse that caused much of the world to erupt in gunfire, explosions, and flame. To this day, no one can conclusively explain why such bestial warfare was the result of the assassination. Historians try their best, plodding their way through a maze of treaties that required one country to come to the defense of another when it was attacked, and in the process causing peaceable intentions to

248

tumble over like dominoes in a row. For instance, consider the analysis of historian Paul Johnson. After the archduke was assassinated, Johnson relates, there followed:

> the Austrian ultimatum to Serbia, the Russian decision to support the Serbs, the French decision to support Russia, the German decision to support Austria and fight a two-front war against Russia and France, and Germany's consequential decision to send its armies through Belgium to enforce quick defeat on the French, and so the involvement of Britain and its dominion allies in support of Belgium.

It is hard to tell whether Johnson is writing an accurate description of the events that led to the massive scale of the war, which he was successful in accomplishing, or a parody of international relations at the time, which he was also successful in accomplishing. Either way, a study of the results of the Great War leads to but one conclusion: the carnage was out of all proportion to the cause, resulting in, as Johnson put it, "the primal tragedy of modern world civilization, the main reason why the 20th century turned into such a disastrous epoch for mankind."

In the United States, which was never a battleground, the conflict nonetheless produced a "lost generation" of men and women, people who struggled to find a purpose in life, a faith to replace the belief in mankind's better nature that had been destroyed by the war's senselessness and brutality. In England there was a more literal kind of lost generation, as the nation suffered so many casualties that, by the war's end, the majority of its young men in their late teens and early to mid-twenties would no longer be alive — lost, in this case, to eternity. Other European countries also suffered the deaths of many of those who could have led them in the future: government officials, scientists, inventors, artists, novelists, historians, academics, builders, investors — appalling proportions of their youth sacrificed to the darker motives of political alliance or uncaring governmental behavior.

President Wilson's first reaction to the archduke's assassination was to insist that it was Europe's business and Europe's alone. He declared that the United States would not get involved. We would tend to our own affairs, remain neutral. Over and over again, the president stuck to his avowal.

Among those who initially supported him was Theodore Roosevelt. It did not seem like a very Rooseveltian thing to do, but the former resident of the White House was, after all, getting on in years and perhaps, some observers thought, combat was losing its appeal.

Not a chance.

Within a few months, as the violence escalated abroad, Roosevelt decided that Wilson was a little *too* neutral. The proper response to the European fighting, he declared, would be to send a message to the Central Powers, as Germany, the Ottoman Empire, the Austro-Hungarian Empire, and the Kingdom of Bulgaria were being called. Having already invaded Belgium and slaughtered hundreds of innocents, the Central Powers were now massing at the borders of other European nations, the so-called Allies, and Roosevelt wanted them to know that the United States would not tolerate such belligerence.

But he would have couched the warning in what was for him atypically muted language. "If I had been President," he told his friend Cecil Spring-Rice, the British ambassador to Washington, "I should have acted on the thirtieth or thirty-first of July, as head of a signatory power to the Hague treaties, calling attention to the guaranty of Belgium's neutrality and saying that I accepted the treaties as imposing a serious obligation which I expected not only the United States but all other neutral nations to join in enforcing. Of course I would not have made such a statement unless I was willing to back it up."

Over the next two years, through much of 1916, Roosevelt became — verbally, at least — not only willing but eager to back it up. The Central Powers showed no signs of becoming less aggressive, no signs of being more receptive to the requests, then the demands, of those who opposed their armed hostilities. It was time, Roosevelt now believed, with too much slaughter already having taken place and no end in sight, for the United States to act.

But that did not mean resorting to weapons, not just yet. This was still the ex-president's view and it was still atypical for him, not to mention self-contradictory, since he secretly, and perversely, admired the war. "The storm that is raging in Europe at this moment is terrible and evil," he wrote privately at an earlier stage of the conflict, "but it is also grand and noble."

It is a puzzling statement. "Terrible and evil" does not fit with "grand and noble"; it seemed that war and peace were waging a struggle within Roosevelt and that the former was gradually gaining ground. Then again, how could it not? Theodore Roosevelt contemplating war was like a miser contemplating riches, a lothario contemplating a beauty pageant; the reaction was instinctive, not a carefully considered decision. He believed that the United States would occupy the battlefield; it was just a matter of time. In fact, he had predicted it, if only by implication, in a letter to Quentin written a little more than a month after Ferdinand's assassination. "The situation in Europe is really dreadful," he told his boy, "and a great tragedy impends." A great tragedy, Quentin knew, could only be met with an outburst of violence. And, old enough now, Quentin realized that, if there were to be such a thing, he would be part of it.

A few months later, with tragedy begetting more tragedy in Europe, Roosevelt added poignantly that it was a war for which "no man could buy a substitute; no man would be excepted because of his wealth; all would serve in the ranks on precisely the same terms side by side."

It seemed a strange comment to make. Few people alive at the time knew of the Civil War practice of paying a person to fight in one's place. But Theodore was speaking to his father; and if he had still been at his son's side, the sire would have agreed.

Rather than making his predictions of war public, Roosevelt became one of the country's leading advocates of "preparedness," which is to say that the United States, although not at the moment headed for combat zones, should be training its troops to undertake such missions. It should also be declaring to nations both friend and foe that it was readying itself for battle and would not be deterred. It should be manufacturing weapons and means of transport, mapping out strategies, deciding on logistics, stiffening its backbone. Only by taking such steps, Roosevelt argued in *Outlook,* could Americans keep Germany and its accomplices at bay and, as a result, help to "create international conditions which shall neither require nor permit such action [as Germany's] in the future."

The Central Powers were undaunted by the prospect of American intervention. If anything, they stepped up the pace of their brutalities, inflicting more losses than ever on the Allies, which included Belgium, France, Italy, Greece, Russia, China, Japan, and Great Britain, among others. As a result, there soon came a point when, although the Allies would not publicly admit it, they found it almost impossible to see any military end for themselves save defeat, utter submission.

And so Roosevelt, conciliatory no more, demanded the end of preparedness, the beginning of war. He had worked his way up to advocacy with uncharacteristic carefulness and reason, he believed — and in truth, for him, he had. But he now believed there was no longer a choice.

At about this time, he left *Outlook* to become an editor at another publication, *Metropolitan* magazine, and had also begun writing nationally syndicated newspaper columns urging the president to send American fighting men to Europe. His criticisms of Wilson for not heeding him turned more and more bitter. The man was "yellow," Roosevelt charged. He was a "molly-coddle pacifist." He was "a timid man, physically." He was "neither a gentleman nor a real man." Privately, Roosevelt wrote that the president was a "skunk" and a "prize jackass." No journalist attacked Wilson as Roosevelt attacked him. One can only imagine what Taft must have thought.

In fact, so abusive was Roosevelt's language that many people, regardless of their positions on the war, were offended, some even writing or speaking to Roosevelt to tell him so. Wilson, they believed, should not be subjected to such abuse, no matter how great one's disagreement with him; the language that Roosevelt was using denigrated the office as well as the man and thus struck at the foundations of democracy. If anyone should know that, Roosevelt should. And, of course, he did, but it had no influence on him. He would not let it. During his own tenure in the White House, Theodore had been a figure of consensus; now, it seemed, he was pure contentiousness.

2

Early in 1917, with the United States still on the sidelines of the Great War, Roosevelt decided that one of the first U.S. fighting men to be sent to Europe should be himself. He was closing in on sixty. *No one* closing in on sixty goes to battle — especially not a man who has recently offered to give up his life in the jungles of South America, and who has lost much of his weight, strength, and will.

Details, Roosevelt thought, mere details. Besides, they were in the past now, and with the archduke's assassination he was feeling more like the old bull moose than ever. In fact, after he had taken Edith for "a wonderful row, far, far out into the Sound," she pronounced her spouse "fine and hearty." It was the first time in a long time that Edith could honestly have made such a statement. It is unlikely, though, that she would have gone so far as to mistake him for the old bull moose again.

But even if he wasn't as fine and hearty as he had been when younger, what did it matter? He was still Colonel Roosevelt, hero of the San Juan Hills, and what he had lost in physical vigor over the years he had gained in experience and knowledge, which would make him an even more valuable leader of troops and master of strategy.

In fact, only a few months after the archduke was killed, and when Theodore's public pronouncements were still restrained, he was already envisioning a "Roosevelt Division" for a new war. It was not the first time he had thought of a Rough Riders Redux. In 1910, he had written to President Taft, offering to raise a troop of cavalry "such as the regiment I commanded in Cuba," in the event of conflict with Mexico or Japan. As it turned out, there was no conflict. Nor was there any desire on Taft's part to have Roosevelt mount up and gallop into the headlines again.

Now, however, there *was* conflict. Deadly and pervasive, the most violent of Roosevelt's lifetime — and his fancy broke free of all its shackles. As if he were "a dreaming boy, he was listing the men he would take with him [to Europe], young army officers who had come to his attention, older ones who had been companions of his in the Spanish-American War, young civilians who begged to be taken as privates."

In time, Theodore began to speak of his dreams, only to a few and only with a minimum of carefully chosen words — but that was enough. A Roosevelt Division! Rumors began to spread, to gain momentum, first by word of mouth, then by items in newspapers and magazines, which only encouraged more word of mouth, more speculation in print. Theodore did not seem upset. In fact, it might have been what he had intended all along, for the result was that "tens of thousands of adventurous youths pleaded for a chance to fight under him; at the peak, applications poured in at the rate of two thousand a day."

Such a spectacular response to a figment of the imagination.

But did Roosevelt really believe he was up to the Great War? It is not certain, and his indecision is fascinating to contemplate. "If I am allowed to go, I could not last," he admitted to his sister and the French ambassador to the United States, with whom he was having tea at the time, a time when the Roosevelt Division was on the minds of so many young men. "I should *crack* but I *could* arouse the belief that America was coming." Pause, then ominously: "What difference would it make if I cracked or not?" It was a strange, almost surreal admission, and made so by more than just the words; it was the tone in which he spoke them, one that had a knowing, fatalistic quality to it.

Roosevelt did not explain what he meant by "cracked." Apparently, neither his sister nor the ambassador bothered to ask.

Nonetheless, Theodore called President Wilson's office in early 1917 for an appointment — at what cost to his pride, his self-respect, the placidity of his gastric juices, one can only guess. But it had to be done, he believed, and he was not a man, his was not a family, to shirk even the most odious of duties. Of which none, he believed, could be more odious than this.

It is not certain how many times Roosevelt had entered the White House since dwelling there, but he had surely never done so under circumstances like these, as a beggar more than a former head of state. He did not bother looking around at once-familiar corridors and walls and artifacts. He did not seek out people he knew, did not check on the condition of poor Mrs. Hayes's lower extremities. Rather, chin tucked down to his chest, lips sealed over those glorious teeth of his, he tramped along a familiar pathway to the president's office and, upon being permitted to enter, kept the small talk to a minimum. He asked Taft's successor for permission to raise a band of volunteers that he would personally lead into battle in France. As president himself, he had won the Nobel Peace Prize. Now, it appeared, he wanted to atone for it.

Wilson, who was gracious even to allow his tormenter's visit, was not surprised. He was also, to say the least, unenthusiastic. He reminded Roosevelt that he had no intention of *any* American leading troops into battle, in France or anywhere else. The United States was still a neutral, and Wilson would do all he could to keep it that way.

Roosevelt plowed on as if he hadn't heard. There was support for the idea of his return to war not only in this country, he pointed out, but overseas as well. The Roosevelt Division would be especially welcome in France, whose premier, Georges Clemenceau, had already written about the matter to Wilson. "At the present moment," Clemenceau stated, "there is in France one name which sums up the beauty of American intervention — Roosevelt. You are too much of a philosopher to ignore that the influence on the people of great leaders of men often exceeds their personal merits. The name Roosevelt has this legendary force in this country at this time. Our poilus [lower-ranking French soldiers] ask, 'Where is Roosevelt?' Send them Roosevelt — it will gladden their hearts."

It would not gladden Wilson's. He repeated to Roosevelt that the war was Europe's affair and would stay that way until the last shot was fired. Of course, even if, through totally unforeseen circumstances, it became America's affair as well, he was certainly not about to call on senior citizens to take up arms — a point Wilson probably did not bring up. He would especially not call on the senior citizen now before him, which he also kept to himself. He gave Roosevelt his hearing, then falsely assured him that should the situation change, he would certainly consider Roosevelt's request and get back to him.

The former president could not help but seethe at Wilson's lack of enthusiasm, his effete mannerisms. But he did so inwardly; outwardly, he thanked the Commander-in-Chief and, with all the dignity he could contrive, took his leave from the White House.

Actually, Wilson did consider Roosevelt's notion — or, rather, allowed the military to do so. He sent a note about their meeting to the famed General John J. "Black Jack" Pershing, who would become, second only to George Washington, the highest-ranking military official in American history. Wilson knew that Pershing shared his opinion of Roosevelt, that he was more bluster than substance, and more of a nuisance than either. And so he knew how Pershing would react to the former president's proposal — by throwing Wilson's notice of it into the wastebasket. The two men must have shared a laugh, and a derisive one, at that. The Roosevelt Division was disbanded before it formed.

As for Wilson, it was a rare light moment in an increasingly worrisome time. He was surely pleased at being able to avenge himself on his most unremitting critic, this old man who still thought himself young enough for war. Within a few days he wrote to Roosevelt, perfunctorily, thanking him for his interest, repeating his commitment to non-intervention, and informing him that, unfortunately, the military had no interest in him. "I really think the best way to treat Mr. Roosevelt is to take no notice of him," Wilson later said, going on to explain that doing so would be "the best punishment that can be exacted." There would be no molly-coddling of the man who had so publicly, and frequently, insulted him.

3

Of course, later that year, with the Allies continuing to flounder in Europe and the lives of numerous civilians having been lost at sea, Wilson would be forced to change his mind. He probably sensed the inevitability of the change as early as 1915, when the British luxury liner *Lusitania* departed from New York, bound for Liverpool. It never got there. German submarines, called U-boats, attacked the ship and sent 1,198 passengers and crew members to the bottom of the ocean floor, lifeless. The cries for American involvement in the fighting crescendoed.

On April 6, 1917, Wilson announced that the United States would enter the conflict after all, and Roosevelt spewed out incendiary versions of "I told you so" in all forums that would have him — and, at this point, virtually all forums would.

Roosevelt also renewed his request for his own division, this time advertising it to the newspapers before forwarding it to Secretary of War Newton D. Baker. When Baker delivered another rejection, its recipient stormed to his writing desk. "My dear sir," he growled to Baker, "you forget that I have commanded troops in action in the most important battle fought by the United States army during the last half century." He had been turned down for a command, he fumed, while they were being dispensed like toys at Christmas to a myriad of others, young soldiers who did not have "one tenth" of his experience. And Roosevelt was just getting started: his letter to the secretary of war ran on for eighteen fulminating pages! The odds of Baker's having read the entire message, after he got the gist, are minimal.

For others in his family, the military was more receptive. Every member of fighting age enlisted, all four of them, with Quentin dropping out of Harvard his sophomore year to do so. None needed his father to tell him to sign up, none had any reservations. "Golden Lads," the boys' sister Ethel called them — and that they were, as they prepared to head off to the Great War. It was their chance to make their father proud of them in the way he would most appreciate, their chance to start compiling the bedtime stories they would one day tell their own children.

Roosevelt confessed his apprehension at first. It was a lot to ask of one family, the possibility of sacrificing so many lives. But he could not allow himself to think in those terms. He quickly shook off his doubts and announced in a letter to Quentin that "the feeling [of reluctance] has now been completely swallowed by my immense pride in all four of you."

And so it was that in this unexpected manner, along this unforeseen trail, Theodore Roosevelt would find escape from the wilderness in which he had been dwelling for so many years. His freedom would be vicarious. So would his militarism. It would simply have to do.

Ted and Archie were commissioned as officers and dispatched to France, where they served with the First Infantry Division. Kermit, "his constitutional weakness for drink" becoming more pronounced all the time, was nonetheless able to join the British troops fighting the Turks in Mesopotamia, although he would later be assigned to

France as well.

As for Quentin, although he much preferred Harvard to Groton, he preferred the battlefield to both. There was something about the very notion of formal education to which he could not seem to adjust. On one occasion, when taking a math test, he found himself making the bizarre transition to verse.

How can I work when my brain is whirling?
What can I do if I've got the grippe?
Why make a bluff at a knowledge that's
    lacking?
What is the use if I don't give a nip?

The poem, which had three stanzas following, would have gotten a better mark in Quentin's sophomore writing class than it did in math. Why he interrupted his equations to break into verse is a puzzle that not even the young man himself could likely solve.

But there were times when his brain was not whirling, and he took to his studies more diligently than ever before. Without Peabody or somebody like him breathing down his neck, he seemed more consistently enthusiastic about learning. He read his class assignments, read the extra-credit work, even read for his own stimulation and satisfaction. "His room was strewn with volumes of prose and poetry — histories, essays, novels, epic poems and detective stories; while what he did had often a touch of the same catholic and individual taste." He was a young man rapidly and responsibly maturing.

And when he wasn't immersed in learning, Quentin was even more diligently falling in love. He had first begun to notice Flora Payne Whitney when she was Archie's girlfriend. A goblin-slayer if ever there was one, Miss Whitney was two years older than Quentin, and her pedigree dazzled: the great-granddaughter of Cornelius Vanderbilt, whose admitted insanity in the cause of wealth had made him hundreds of millions in shipping and railroads; the granddaughter of Cornelius Vanderbilt II, president of the New York Central Railroad and a multimillionaire himself; the daughter of H. P. Whitney, who had "inherited one fortune, married another, and amassed a third" — all of them figures of "superhuman stinginess," to repeat Mark Twain's assessment.

But Flora was also the daughter of the woman who had founded the Whitney Museum of American Art, and it was her mother after whom she most took. Flora was "slender, dark-haired, a lovely young woman who was not only attractive but intelligent, self-possessed and cheery."

For some reason, lost to time, her relationship with Archie did not last. Quentin was at the head of the line when it ended. He could not have been more wisely smitten, and Archie seemed genuinely pleased to have passed Flora along.

Before the United States entered the war, Quentin and his "Fouf," as he called her, had talked about the conflict often as they strolled along the banks of Cambridge's Charles River, the campus on one side of them, the Harvard crew practicing on the other — so far from the European violence. But he made it clear that, if America ever became a combatant, he would sign up. It was his duty, he told her. Flora assured him that she understood, and would wait for him as long as necessary.

Quentin's zeal for combat was growing, but one night, as he sat in his dorm room alone thinking about the possible outcomes of combat, he wrote Flora a note that might have been dictated by the goblin at the headboard. "I don't see why people should worry so over their death. I suppose I'm very old-fashioned, but I've always been sure that there was something beyond that I didn't know about, and consequently I've never spent any time worrying over whether God is or there is a life hereafter. I must be a throw-back to the agnostic times.

"— Whoa! I'm getting much too complicated — and I'm a little uncertain as to what you'll say about this."

Before long, Quentin and Flora would be writing farewell letters to each other, she pleading with her future husband not to "take any unnecessary risks — or do anything solely for bravado — please, please, dear?"

His reply is not known, but, sincerely or not, it was surely intended to put her mind at ease.

However, he had come to a decision, albeit a pointless one, that would not have put her mind at ease had she known of it. He had determined that if there were a God, and He chose just one of the Roosevelt brothers to die in battle, it should be he. The others all had wives and children, even though Archie's heir was still in utero; Quentin was thus, by his own reasoning, the most expendable of the Golden Lads. It did not seem to bother him.

The war was an obvious obstacle to Quentin's romance. Flora's father might have been a greater one. Harry Payne Whitney could not have been more opposed to the union of his daughter and a young man whose future seemed certain to be interrupted by a year or two under fire. And, to make matters worse, if preposterously so, he was a young man whose father was nothing more than a freelance writer and editor earning, at best, about $30,000 a year, a sum that "would not have defrayed half the cost of one of H. P. Whitney's regular grouse shoots on the moors of England." That the writer had also been Assistant Secretary of the Navy, Governor of New York, Vice President of the United States, and then President of the United States for almost two terms, did not matter to people to whom money was the sole measure of the man. Even at his peak, Roosevelt was but a public official; as far as H. P. Whitney was concerned, H. P. Whitney and family were royalty, hardly mere "public," and thus answerable to no elected official.

Flora, however, ignored her father's snobbery. In fact, it had been a practice of hers to ignore it for years. When she made her debut in New York society, it was Quentin Roosevelt's arm to which she clung, and both of his arms that held her as she "danced all night, then took a sunrise dip in the sea." And when she decided she wanted to marry, it was Quentin she intended for her spouse. Quentin's intention was joyously identical. H. P.'s intentions were irrelevant.

Yet Quentin hesitated. He could not at first bear the thought of leaving either Flora *or* Harvard, but once his enlistment became a certainty, he could not make up his mind whether to marry before he was sent to action or after he returned.

In truth, he should not have seen action at all. Quentin's vision was so poor that the only way he could pass an eye test was to get a copy of the chart beforehand and memorize the positions of the letters. His back was so bothersome that there were times when he could not sleep, times when it pained him even to rise from a chair. And he was still subject to his various illnesses, seemingly at whim. Had he been anyone but a Roosevelt, he would have failed his physical and been sent back to campus.

But, Wilson's and Pershing's feelings about the senior Roosevelt notwithstanding, Quentin received preferential treatment by recruiters and physicians alike. Not only did he pass his exam, as had his brothers before him, he was regarded as officer material.

His love for his Fouf notwithstanding, he could not wait to begin serving his country, and he immediately decided on "the most adventurous and tenuous new military service, the army air corps." He had never been in a plane before, however, and it was not until his first flight that Quentin discovered he was beset by yet another malady, this one seemingly the most troublesome of all for a pilot: airsickness.

But the Army Air Corps was not as strange a choice as it seemed. Quentin had always "loved heights, and the eagle's-eye perception that height endows." As a child, he had had a fondness for models, miniature versions of landscapes over which he could tower. Perhaps his favorite was a model of the nation's capital. "Look down on the White House," he said when he was living there, "as if you were a god! How small it looks. . . . You could drop a pebble on it and crush it, together with the p-i-g-m-y president and the State-War-Navy Department, too, by mistake."

As if experimenting on ways to challenge gravity, Quentin had spent a disproportionate amount of his childhood hanging upside down from tree limbs, standing on his head, "or reclined in a chair with his feet comfortably resting where his head should normally be." And once, as Earle Looker remembered about the old White House Gang days, Quentin persuaded a man who owned a new roadster to take the boys for a ride. It was the first time any of them had been in an automobile, and they were exhilarated. "We're speed demons!" Quentin shouted at the passing landscape. "This must be exactly like flying!"

Shortly after that, he bought his first model plane, "one which can fly a hundred yards, and goes higher than my head." And before that, even before he had been captivated by the aeroplanes gliding higher than his head in France, he had chosen "A Trip on an Airship" as the title of a paper he was assigned at Episcopal High School, to which he and Archie had matriculated after Force, in Washington.

My airship is my own invention. Its balloon which holds hydrogen gas is 25 feet long. The boat below the balloon is 15 feet long and at its widest 2 feet. It has a 24 horsepower 6 cylinder Packard engine and carries a tank which has a cubic capacity of 200 yd. It has a rudder capable of steering it up or downward and is propelled by a screw.

On Monday, June 20 at ten o'clock I started from Washington. I passed a number of cities and at 6 o'clock reached New York.

My opinion is that airships will sometime be a success.

The journey of which he wrote was, of course, imaginary. His forthcoming flights would not be.

Quentin took much of his flight training near the Roosevelts' Sagamore Hill home on Long Island, at a field that would one day bear his name in tribute. But he was not in the air as much as he hoped to be. The American military had entered the war so suddenly, and so late, that it was not ready for it — not enough rifles, not enough machine guns, not enough ammunition, not enough uniforms, and, most frustrating to Quentin, not enough aircraft.

Prepare, prepare, his father had exhorted a few years ago, back when there had actually been time to prepare. His government had not listened, and Wilson had thereby assured what Roosevelt would have delighted in calling The Second War of America the Unready.

Still, Quentin managed his share of hours

in the cockpit, and during most of them he thrilled to be soaring through the clouds, exhilarated by his newfound mastery of the skies. But more often, at least at the start of training, his airsickness plagued him, especially after he landed. He was unsteady, nauseous, the kind of feeling that a roller coaster inflicts on a person whose stomach is not up to the challenge, who feels the earth wobble beneath his feet when he steps onto it again. He told no one about this, not directly, at least. To his mother, however, he freely discussed his related maladies. "I did three hours and a half yesterday," he wrote, "and over four hours to-day. I have been having a continual fight with the doctors, tho, and incidentally with myself. The trouble is that I have been getting in so much flying lately that I am tired out most of the time. The net result was that I collected another cough, as my lung wasn't quite fixed up. I had been feeling rather poorly, but I was pretty anxious to get my flying done, so I was keeping on."

No one was more puzzled by this than he. His mind wanted to fly. His body, apparently, had occasional doubts. How to resolve such a problem? "Aviation has considerably altered my views on religion," he wrote home on December 8, 1917, still not overtly admitting his problem. "I don't see how the angels stand it."

Early in 1918 he was transferred from Long Island to Washington, D.C., where his indoctrination took a decidedly sadistic turn. According to Alice, who was infuriated by Quentin's reports, his superiors "poured hot and cold water into his ears, filled his eyes with belladonna, and made him hop about while blindfolded." These tortures, bizarrely administered by those in charge of his welfare, were supposed to determine a pilot's ability to withstand such treatment should he happen to be captured. When Quentin had established to the satisfaction of the Army Air Corps that he was up to such challenges, he received his orders. He would join his brothers. He would board a ship, for the first time since he was twelve, with France once again his destination.

The night before his departure was spent at Sagamore Hill. Just like old times, except not like old times at all. He found himself oddly uncomfortable, more so than he had ever been before at home. Was it because his parents were working so hard, and ineffectively, at cheerfulness? As for the house itself, he loved it as much as ever, gloomy though it had always appeared. He knew

276

every inch of it, every carpet and corner, every floorboard — having so many years ago crawled so extensively over them. He knew every animal head and its precise location, every painting on the walls, and every step up to the second and third floors, where the servants lived and where his father had a private retreat he called his Gun Room.

Yet in a matter of hours he would leave all that was familiar behind, much farther behind than it had been when he was at school. And so to sit at Sagamore on his last night in America, to look around at the setting that had so defined him, led to ineffable sadness.

Small talk remained an effort for the three of them during a late dinner, and continued to be a struggle after they removed themselves, drinks in hand, to the North Room, an addition to the original, built under the Roosevelts' supervision, in 1905. The parents and child seemed lost in the space. Quentin had already said his tearful goodbyes to Flora; for some reason, he decided not to tell his parents that they had become engaged.

After a few minutes, he made his apologies, said he was tired and needed his rest for tomorrow. His parents agreed, and not without relief. They, too, were depressingly ill at ease. He walked over to his father and hugged him. Theodore returned the embrace so tightly that he almost took the breath out of his boy; disengaging, and then Quentin nodded a few times and tramped slowly upstairs. A few minutes more and he was in bed, his mother entering his room and adjusting the covers around him, tucking the blanket and sheet snugly under his chin and smoothing it — just the way she used to do a long time ago and for that reason an act that was simultaneously soothing and awkward for them both. Edith kissed him goodnight and departed.

She "was later to admit that she found his going very, very hard, but, at the same time, she realized the truth in the expression that 'you can't bring up boys to be eagles and expect them to turn out sparrows.' "

The next morning brought stiff upper lips, final good-byes, and an early departure. Now all four of the Roosevelt boys were officially at war or on their way.

The silence at Sagamore Hill was like a weight that the shoulders of the two residents could barely support.

Upon arriving overseas, Quentin found himself precisely where he did not want to be: far from the action. His primary duties with the 95th Aero Squadron consisted of supply and reconnaissance missions that were carried out well beyond the reach, or even interest, of the Central Powers. His ability to speak French made him valuable for such tasks and thus proved to be a curse. His days, he said, were of a "uniform & appalling dullness."

One of the ways he tried to relieve it was by boxing, a common sporting pastime for the men of the 95th. Unfortunately, he fared little better in the ring than his father had, less than a decade earlier, Quentin was a flailer, not a fighter; he would swing wildly, defend himself poorly. After one match, he had to tell his mother that "yesterday I succeeded in getting one on the nose which the Doctor thinks may have broken it. It doesn't look crooked, tho, so I think he may be wrong."

Safer to pick up his pen again, he decided, although his mother would have been even less gratified to read his sketch, "The Greatest Gift," than she was to learn of his boxing mishap. As far as is known, he never showed the piece to anyone. It was not an assignment of any kind; he was beyond academic duties now. Apparently it was just something he was thinking about, and so incessantly that he needed the release of setting it down on paper. An excerpt:

> Death, whom I had cursed, seemed not a kindly friend, who, when we tire of our toys, and all our little mortal playthings are faded and broken, comes soft-handed to heal all with his dreamless quiet.
> And within me my soul cried out: "Yes. Ah, yes! Death, death and oblivion are God's greatest gifts."

Quentin's goblin just kept following him, now all the way to France.

While Theodore's youngest was morbidly musing, flying through empty skies, his brothers were on the front lines risking their lives. To them, or so they said, their youngest sibling was "a slacker, unworthy of the Roosevelt name." They were teasing, of course, but with an unmistakable edge — and Quentin did not see the humor. To the contrary, he felt that Ted and Kermit, and in this case even Archie, were ganging up on him, and Quentin had no patience for it. Perhaps he thought back to other such occasions, most notably the time when his brothers taunted him to jump off the cliff into the cove near Oyster Bay, and he had done so fearfully.

But he was not fearful now. Quentin was as eager for battle as his siblings, and when it came he would comport himself just as commendably. He could not understand why his unit continued to be given such mundane assignments, so far away from the peril that was the very definition of war.

He grew more and more morose. Previously, he had suffered a bout of pneumonia, the result of high-altitude training, more reason to wonder about his decision to take to the air. During this period, this most epistolary of the young Roosevelts stopped writing letters home. He might have had the time, but he was curiously lacking in desire.

The silence was hard on those he left behind, especially Theodore, who had trouble sleeping, and when awake was struck once again by the return of his own ailments: Cuban malaria, his infected leg — they had become old friends by now. In fact, when his boys were abroad, Roosevelt added new bodily malfunctions to his previous list: rectal abscesses, fistulas, sepsis, rheumatism, and anemia. The old warrior was fighting his own battles, and his foes were in their own way just as vicious as the Hun. He was within two years of sixty. Perhaps his body was preparing itself.

Eventually, journalists found out about the state of Theodore's health. Reports slowly made their way across the ocean and his sons wrote as soon as they could to express their concern. Even Quentin snapped out of his lethargy to communicate. Roosevelt wrote back promptly, dispatching letters to each of the young Roosevelt soldiers assuring them that the press accounts had been exaggerated. It was not true. If anything, they had been understated, but Theodore would not be a distraction to his children, would not allow them to worry about him. He blamed the stories of his ill health on sensation-seeking newspapers. His boys, with enough troubles of their own — and on a mission in their father's stead, so to speak — allowed themselves to be convinced.

They should not have been. Roosevelt was actually reaching a nadir and, although it was kept a secret from as many in the family as possible, he had to be hospitalized for a time. What a bullet had not accomplished in Milwaukee, a parasite, dormant for a time, had accomplished in South America.

And so weakened had the former president become that some of the letters he wrote to his boys, insisting on his robustness, cursing irresponsible reporters, not only came from a hospital room, but were partially written by Ethel; her husband needed a hand in guiding the pen.

"In fact," according to Peter Collier and David Horowitz, "the illness was so bad — both ears were deeply infected and the abscesses that had tormented him periodically since the Brazil trip had reappeared — that at one point he believed he was dying and roused himself from a deep fever to whisper what he thought might be his last words . . . : 'I am so glad that it is not one of my boys who is dying here, for *they* can die for their country.'" He still believed, as he had done half a century earlier, staring into the abyss, that when the end of all sensations came, there was a certain glory to the battlefield as scenario.

After having inquired about his father's maladies, Quentin wrote again, this time seeking consolation from Theodore for his brothers' derision. In reply, he received a message that buoyed his feelings greatly. The message does not survive; but at about the same time that he received it, Quentin had managed to procure a typewriter; he was able to reply without having to depend on his sloppy handwriting.

Dearest Father,

Thanks very much for the cable. I just got it yesterday, and it's such a relief to know that you do understand and that you don't think I am hedging because I'm not yet up there. . . .

I've got to leave now, for flying, so I'm going to quit. I love hearing from you, for though it seems a queer thing to say, it's pleasant to hear a little of what is going on at home instead of a set of glowing generalities about what we are about to do! Most of the people at home don't seem to have the least conception of what we're up against over here. . . .

Another letter coming as soon as I can get the time. Best love to all the family, dearest father, from

Your loving son,
Quent.

His mind did not rest easy for long. Making him feel all the guiltier for not having seen action yet was news that Archie had been the victim of enemy fire, also in France but many miles away. According to the report Quentin received, his brother had been in a great deal of pain "as the surgeon pried a large chunk of shrapnel from his left femur and tweezed smaller fragments from his left humerus, which was splintered and broken in two places."

In addition, Archie had been exposed to mustard gas, a noxious vapor that made its unfortunate debut in World War I. It raised blisters almost immediately on exposed skin and, if inhaled, could form them on the lungs as well. Like Quentin with one of his backaches, Archie's various injuries made it virtually impossible for him to find a comfortable configuration in which to sleep; usually he had to settle for propping himself up with pillows in an overstuffed chair. It would work for a while, then he would awaken himself with spasms of coughing.

Quentin was allowed to visit his brother in April 1918 and found the sight of him alarming. "He is very thin," Quentin wrote home, "and is in this horrid position now of not knowing what is going to happen to him."

The youngest brother could not stay with Archie as long as he had hoped, his squadron demanding his presence again after what amounted to little more than a long weekend. But he returned in a troubled frame of mind, and only after asking that Archie's doctors and superior officers keep him informed of his condition. They assured him they would. Quentin was not assuaged.

Later, ironically, the war would inflict the same indignities on Ted, although to a lesser degree. He would receive a single shrapnel wound and pick up the scent of mustard gas from afar. He had a much easier time recovering.

Archie's condition would remain virtually the same throughout the summer, and in September he would be discharged from active duty with full disability. His soldiering days, it seemed, were over.

But, to the surprise of no one more than he, they were not. Some of his injuries healed more quickly than his doctors had anticipated, some more thoroughly, and he would gradually, though never fully, recover. Despite the fact that he would see no more combat in the Great War, he would be cleared to fight again in World War II, a miraculous occurrence for someone once dismissed from the service for his infirmities. Then again, he felt he owed his country for the time he'd missed in the previous conflict, and the name of the president who

286

allowed him to make up for it was, of course, Roosevelt. Archie was dispatched to the Pacific, where, under the reign of General Douglas MacArthur, he conducted himself so admirably that he earned a Silver Star with Oak Leaf Clusters. The former is the third highest award given by the United States for gallantry in battle; the latter, the oak leaves, denote that the recipient has won the award twice. Archie demonstrated such courage while fighting in New Zealand that the Australian soldiers with whom he served named a peak they had conquered "Roosevelt Ridge," a second cartographic honor for the family. "At one point," wrote Collier and Horowitz, "he was in combat continuously for seventy-six days" — and this was a man approaching his fiftieth birthday!

Eventually, Theodore made an unexpected recovery too, from both his delirium and his physical afflictions, at least enough to be released from the hospital and sent back to Sagamore Hill. Waiting for him there was Ethel; having seen to it that all was in order for the master's return, she now seemed to have found a purpose in life stronger than she had ever known before. Roosevelt had always adored his younger daughter, the baby doll come to life. But he did not know her nearly as well as her mother did. It was with his four boys, not the girl born two years after Kermit, that he shared so many interests, probably making it inevitable that he would love her more than know her. And since, unlike her stepsister, Ethel was a woman of low maintenance, seemingly born to nurture and almost always in good spirits, she had never frustrated her father as Alice had, which is to say that she never demanded as much of his time or energy. But now, Ethel felt, it was time to step to the fore. Moving into Sagamore with her husband, surgeon Richard Derby, and their two infant children, she told Edith she was off duty, could finally rest; from now on, Ethel would take control of recuperative efforts for her father, providing many of them herself and supervising the family members and nurses who assisted her.

Her father was not the most compliant of patients. He "often managed to annoy the nurses hired by Ethel and his daughters-in-law by making unscheduled trips to the nursery where he waited until no one was looking and then woke up his infant grand-children so he could hold them."

But, for the most part, it was Ethel who managed to annoy Theodore; she insisted that he rest far more than he wanted to, that he take medicine more often than he wanted to, and that he cross the hallway to see his grandchildren less than he wanted to, and only when assisted by a nurse. Sagamore Hill was Ethel's house now, more than it had ever been when she was a little girl; and for several months after her father departed from the hospital, she ran it with a degree of tender efficiency that benefited all under her command, including her weary and continually fretful mother.

5

At last, in late May 1918, the wait was over. The 95th Aero Squadron received its orders to report to the front, and Quentin was as surprised as he was ecstatic. "Cheers, oh cheers," he cabled home, sounding like a child who has just received the birthday present he most wanted, "and I'm very happy." His father realized that, because of his son's youth, his "part is one of peculiar honor and peril," and he began to worry again. To Quentin, however, he relayed only optimism. Theodore, having become even healthier by now, was, he told his boy, "thrilled" that he would be getting closer not only to the action, but to the other three Golden Lads. "I know well how hard the long delay has been, when you could have fitted yourself to go to the front six months ago; and my joy for you and pride in you drown out my anxiety."

Roosevelt's joy only increased when he learned that his youngest son was establishing himself as the most respected figure in his squadron. In a letter dispatched to his family at home, one of the men who served under him wrote, "We have a real man commanding us now, just like his father." Another of Quentin's subordinates told his parents, "We boys would do anything for him. He always sees that his men are taken care of before he thinks of himself."

When Roosevelt learned of such encomia, he did so "with swelling chest." To Quentin, he wrote, "All the family are proud as peacocks. . . . My disappointment at not going myself was down at bottom chiefly reluctance to see you four, in whom my heart was wrapped, exposed to danger while I stayed at home in do-nothing ease and safety. But the feeling has now been completely swallowed in my immense pride in all of you. I feel that *Mother,* and all of *you* children, have by your deeds justified *my* words!!!"

Still, something lingered in Theodore, something troubling and not to be admitted. It scarcely needs to be said that his pride was genuine, but it did not drown out his anxiety. He did, after all, so love his children, and now they were emulating his greatest desire, of being soldiers at the front in a grand and glorious struggle. But, somehow, Roosevelt seems never to have thought through the consequences of his wish coming true. Somehow, it was only with his boys' departure for France that the possibility of not all of them returning struck their father. It is reminiscent of his loneliness in Africa, and his not realizing he would miss his family so much until the moment he left them behind. It is reminiscent of a six-year-old's inability to think of the long term. Theodore seems to have found it so much easier to consider the glory of war than the misery that could also be its outcome.

But Archie had already made the sacrifice for the family, hadn't he? And he had survived. The invoice for the Roosevelt family, Theodore wanted to believe, had been marked PAID.

A picture of Quentin at this time, with an unidentified dog at his side, shows a handsome young man, his hair rigidly parted about halfway between the middle of his skull and the side. His shoulders are slumped, his smile uncertain, eyes not fully open. Perhaps he was squinting into the sun, perhaps into the future. There is a shyness in his expression; he could almost be mistaken for a young Lindbergh. One has to look harder for a degree of confidence equal to Lindbergh's.

By now, he had decided that he could wait no longer to marry his Fouf, war or no war. The Whitneys were gradually getting used to the idea of having a mere Roosevelt in the family, and the Roosevelts had long been enamored of their son's beloved, if not her father. Flora visited Theodore often during his illnesses, and one night, after she had come to dinner with the family, he found her "so darling and pretty; and afterwards she wrote [to Edith] one of the finest, dearest letters ever written by a young girl happy in her love but sundered from her lover."

That dinner, in fact, seems to have inspired Roosevelt. "Why don't you write to Flora, and to her father and mother," he told his son via mail, surely not realizing how cold-hearted he was about to sound, surely believing in glory more than misery, "asking if she won't come abroad and marry you? As for your getting killed, or ordinarily crippled, afterwards, why she would rather have married you than not have married you under those conditions; and as for the extraordinary kinds of crippling, they are rare, and anyway we have to take certain chances in life."

The War Department, however, was not in a romantic mood. It denied Flora permission to go overseas at such a dangerous time. It was, thought her prospective father-in-law, an "idiotic ruling" — something unmistakably Wilsonian about it. God, how Theodore had come to loathe that man!

It was no surprise that the Roosevelts depended on letters more than ever with the country at war. The boys' aunts, Bamie and Corinne, wrote to the soldiers almost as much as their parents did, and, save for Quentin's single lapse, the boys wrote home, and to one another, as often as they could. One Roosevelt who would not even be an official Roosevelt until her wedding day might have written most of all. "I got a lot of letters all at once yesterday," Quentin related before he had been ordered to battle, "four from Flora, two from you and two from father. You have no idea what it is to get letters over here and to feel, for a few minutes at least, that home and the U.S.A. are not so very far away. Every now and then I get frightfully gloomy and then the letters help out tremendously."

But the letters did not always come, and certainly did not come often, usually due to the military's inability to handle volumes of mail with which it had never had to deal before. Quentin, however, took the absence of correspondence personally.

Dearest Mother; — Its been five weeks since I've heard from any of the family, so I feel sure I must have committed some horrible crime and be in deep disgrace. From my thoroly black conscience I can find any number of explanations bit [but] the one I feel guiltiest about is that this is the first letter I've written in three weeks. There is some excuse tho' for I have moved all over France in that length of time.

Quentin's captain, the famed air ace and Medal of Honor recipient Eddie Rickenbacker, was dubious about his new recruit at first. He feared that, as the son of a famous man, Quentin would be expecting special treatment, which he was not about to give. He also feared that Quentin might be lacking in necessary skills, that his instructors had gone easy on him and certified him without sufficient cause — and Rickenbacker had no intention of conducting remedial courses.

He was wrong on both counts. After spending no more than two or three days with him, Rickenbacker described Quentin as "hearty and absolutely square in everything he said or did," and years later, in his memoirs, went further. "Quentin Roosevelt was one of the most popular fellows in the group," he told his readers. "We loved him purely for his own natural self."

But after his first few missions, Rickenbacker and the fellows also began to think that this natural self was prone to a frightening recklessness once off the ground. In particular, they might have thought about the day he reduced the 95th's already insufficient number of available aircraft by one. As he wrote to his father, sounding surprisingly light-hearted, he "smashed one plane up beautifully. . . . It was really a very neat job, for I landed with a drift, touched one wing, and then, as there was a high wind, did three complete summersaults (spelling?) ending up on my back. I crawled out of it with nothing more than a couple of scratches."

Quentin blamed the crash on a cold so severe that he could not control the plane;

in fact, the squadron's doctor feared it would lead to another case of pneumonia. Rickenbacker, however, was not in the mood for excuses. He spoke to Quentin about the manner in which he had tempted calamity, and his voice was loud enough to be heard in adjoining tents. Quentin promised to be more careful in the future.

He needed to be. The Americans might not have had enough planes, but the French did not have enough mechanically sound planes, and it was in French planes that Americans flew many of their missions. "They have been in service for ages," Quentin complained to his father, "and have old motors and fuselages and wings that are all warped and bent out of shape."

Theodore must have smiled ruefully, recalling his own complaints about insufficient weaponry during the Spanish-American War. When would his country be ready for war, even eager? Surely the time would have to come, the lesson eventually to be learned. And, less surely, perhaps Roosevelt would finally get the credit he deserved for his advocacy of war. Almost immediately after their summons to the front, Quentin and his mates found themselves under siege, more than Rickenbacker had expected. On average they were losing a man every twenty-four hours, and the "life of a chase pilot on the Front in the summer of 1918 was eleven days." Nor did the Hun show any signs of letting up. "We all went over to the funeral of those two fellows that were killed," Quentin informed his family. "I was flying above it and so I couldn't tell so well. The coffins were escorted by a platoon of American soldiers, and one of French sent out from the French post."

Quentin seemed destined for a coffin of his own before long. In a letter to his parents written by a friend, fellow airman Hamilton Coolidge, he explained a "*coup de main* [that Quentin] sprang today. While on patrol with some eight or nine of his comrades . . . the formation became broken up [and] Q. suddenly found himself alone." Soon he was flying on the tail of three German aircraft. "Sneaking close up behind the rear man who either did not see him or supposed him to be one of his friends, Q. took careful aim and let him have a stream of bullets from his machine gun. The plane wavered a second, then toppled over and fell spinning in a spiral like a winged stone. Q. reversed and headed for home at full speed pursued by two bewildered Huns whom he gradually left further behind. . . . Isn't that one of the most remarkable true tales you have ever heard?"

It was the first German plane Quentin had downed, and he wrote to his Fouf about it as soon as he landed. "I was scared perfectly green," he confessed, "but then I thought to myself that I was so near I might as well take a crack at one of them."

The Roosevelts learned another remarkable tale about their son several days after the fact in a front-page article in the *New York Times.* Quentin "got cut off by a cloud from his fellows, and coming out of the cloud saw three aviators whom he took for Americans. When he got quite close he found they were boche [a derogatory term for Germans], and coolly opened fire on them. All three attacked him, but he got home safe."

Once again, Quentin seemed to be flying recklessly, despite having given his word to Rickenbacker that he would behave himself. It is not known whether the Captain chastised his young aviator again; perhaps he thought it would do no good. If so, he was right. For Quentin seemed to have been born to behave impulsively in the heavens. He had been so courageous as a tree-climbing boy, and later — in France, of all places — became captivated by the skies, wondering what it must be like to sail effortlessly through the open spaces above, riding the wind and looking down on the world, seeing it as the tiny, un-intimidating place that it really was. He had so struggled to find a place for himself since the White House Gang had broken up, to find a similar sense of adventure and team spirit, to find the joy that a classroom could never offer someone as spirited as he. He appeared to have found it in the 95th Squadron, appeared unafraid although there was so much more at stake than playing Kettle Hill with the Gang.

By this time, it had been a while since he had said anything to his parents about airsickness, about failing to understand the appeal of flight to angels. Neither seemed to concern him anymore. Now that he was seeing action, he finally felt like an aviator, master of his body as well as of his aircraft. And as for other aircraft, well, they were far bigger than the letters on an eye chart, and Quentin could see them just fine.

Early in July 1918, he wrote to his parents, intending to share his elation. Instead, and not for the first time, he gave them reason for dread. When you are airborne, he told them, "You get so excited that you forget everything except getting the other fellow."

The action now was unremitting. So was

the peril. A few days after writing the previous letter, Quentin was being pursued by two German pilots while himself in pursuit of another. "I saw my tracers going all around him," Quentin said, "but for some reason he never even turned, until all of a sudden his tail came up and he went down in a vrille [likely a reference to a mysterious yet fictional force described in a novel by Edward Bulwer-Lytton]. I wanted to follow him but the other two [German planes] had started around after me, so I had to cut and run. However, I could half watch him looking back, and he was still spinning when he hit the clouds three thousand meters below."

It was such a long way from pillow fighting to full Rooseveltian manhood, but Quentin had by now achieved it.

He returned to base elated.

His fellow flyers welcomed him back with booze, bravos, and bear hugs.

Rickenbacker shook his hand, beaming at him.

Three days later, on July 14, 1918, he was dead.

FOUR:
THE END OF THE STORY

1

Quentin Roosevelt, flying an American plane that did not malfunction, had been shot down in the French countryside, behind enemy lines. There were conflicting reports about whether his aircraft was on fire as it sped to earth; in all likelihood it was not. There were conflicting reports about whether it dropped as straight as a missile; in all likelihood it was spinning out of control. There was also a report that the crash did not kill him, that he was already dead, having taken two bullets in the head from a German pilot in one of the seven planes that pursued him. This is almost certainly what happened, a remarkable feat of marksmanship from an enemy pilot giving chase through the air.

The Germans in the two planes that had followed Roosevelt earthward landed their aircraft nearby and wiggled out of their

301

cockpits. They approached the wreckage. When they found the body, they searched it for identification, and, discovering the name of the man they had shot out of the skies, found themselves proud and perhaps a touch horrified at the same time. They decided that he should be paid all due respect. It was not the German way, but this was a special case. They returned to their planes for the equipment they needed. Then they "dug a grave, and conducted a military burial service, marking the grave with a cross lettered in English: 'Lieutenant Roosevelt, buried by the Germans, July 14, 1918.'

"A few days later they flew over the line to drop a small bundle containing his effects, which included his identification bracelet, a small metal disk on a silver chain." It landed almost perfectly on the site.

Nothing like this had ever happened before in the Great War, nor was such an act repeated. In the midst of fields full of dead and decomposing bodies and unidentified burial sites, the Germans had erected a memorial to a fallen foe, the only foe to whom they had paid such tribute.

In the last letter his parents received before

his death, reaching them on July 11, 1918, their son had written with customary bravado. "We lost another fellow from our squadron three days ago," he said. "However, you get lots of excitement to make up for it. . . ."

2

Summer at Sagamore Hill. The daisies, as usual, were in full bloom, some of them standing erect, some swaying as narrow streams of wind blew through them, and some limp, having been trampled by deer, mashed to the ground and never to rise. The trees rose tall and deep green behind them. The sun beat down on the grass, browning it in patches despite frequent waterings. It was cut every few days; the scent of newly mown lawn was in the air, crisp and bracing.

Indoors, though, the house was draped in its usual twilight hues and was more silent than it had ever been before, not just because the children didn't live there any longer, but because four of the children were stationed in a war zone, and there was no telling what information their parents might receive on any given day. At any given hour.

Ethel and her nursing corps had departed,

too. Her father would never be the man he used to be, but he had improved enough so that constant supervision was no longer necessary.

Theodore spent most of his time writing: letters, of course, a constant stream of correspondence to all the boys, in addition to tales of their adventures to other members of the family; but also columns on the fighting abroad for a number of publications, columns that almost always took issue with Wilson's strategy or political motivations. He did his work in the library, always alone, usually joining Edith for meals. He avoided most social events and did little public speaking, believing it to be inappropriate during wartime. He did not visit friends as much as he used to, and they were cautious about visiting him, keeping their visits brief and their conversation restricted to small talk.

Edith got out of the house more than her husband, shopping in Oyster Bay and paying calls on friends, sometimes women who also had sons abroad. But she, too, spent a lot of time within Sagamore's walls, especially in her downstairs quarters, a private living room that stood across the front entranceway from the library. The upholstery was brightly colored and patterned; the drapes, usually opened, were white with an almost sparkling blue trim, so that even when closed the ambience was brighter than that of her husband's lair. And all day, no matter how brightly the sun shone in from outside, the electric lights on various tables were turned on, making hers by far the most cheerful room in the house. She would sit at her desk and write her own letters, as well as instructions to the staff, notes to herself about what needed to be done in the days ahead. And she would put down her pen from time to time and drift away to France in her thoughts. It was hard for her to believe she lived in the same world as her son.

The first news about Quentin to reach the estate, from an Associated Press reporter who came to the door, was as ominous as it was unclear. He had brought a telegram with him, one that had just been received at his office. "Watch Sagamore Hill for [censored]," it read. He handed it to Theodore, whom he could not call a friend, but certainly an acquaintance, the two of them having met and talked on numerous professional occasions. Neither Archie nor Ted was in battle at present, and Kermit's unit had temporarily retreated from the front lines. Something had happened to Quentin, the youngest of the Golden Lads. Quentin, Theodore thought; it had to be Quentin.

The Associated Press reporter, Phil Thompson, urged Roosevelt not to worry, assuring him that more information would follow soon and would probably clear up the confusion.

But how?

The next morning, a different Phil Thompson returned and it was obvious he didn't want to. His eyes were on the ground and his footsteps reluctant. He gave off the scent of hesitation. He notified the Roosevelts that their son's plane had been shot down in France. Quentin might have survived and been captured by the Germans. He might have survived and escaped. He might have been injured and at this moment be receiving treatment from either the Allies or Central Powers. And, of course, there was another possibility. His fate, for the time being, was unknown.

All of a sudden, it was as if the clocks at Sagamore Hill had been readjusted by an otherworldly hand; the pace of hours became achingly slow, and the ticking of the old clock in the hallway seemed as loud as the tolling of a church bell. Both Theodore and Edith put aside their pens and came together for mutual support, although it is unlikely they had much to say to each other. There was no point in talking about such indecision as they now faced. They paced, changed rooms, went outside as if looking for someone to come up the driveway with more news. Surely they uttered private prayers. They did not sleep, although they tried, and barely ate. No reporters had gathered outside; there was no such thing as a "death watch" yet in the gentleman's game of American journalism.

Sometimes, when he needed a deeper solitude than his nature had ever required before, a state approaching non-existence, Roosevelt would climb to the third floor and lock himself into the Gun Room, just the old soldier and his own thoughts of what might have happened in France. One imagines an almost Zen-like state. He sat behind his desk in a chair made from the antlers of a Texas longhorn; atop the desk was an inkwell that had once been the foot of a rhinoceros. The room was furnished with rifles in a glass case, swords mounted on one of the walls and musk ox and ram heads on another. On the floor were cougar and Kodiak bearskin rugs.

He used to write some of his books here.

The room was a haven for Roosevelt, a place of contentment — at least at times when contentment was possible. What he did in the room now, no one can say.

As for Edith, she "had been rehearsing this moment ever since that day in 1898 when Theodore had gone off to war. She had relived the feeling any number of times during his presidency when she thought of Lincoln's assassination, and Garfield's, and McKinley's. . . . Her fears had lifted somewhat when they left the White House, only to return redoubled when Theodore was shot in 1912. Now he was safe, but her sons were in danger — and Quentin probably in more than mere danger. Was he dead? Was he dying? It was more than a mother could bear."

The tension, for the Roosevelts at home, the Roosevelts who lived elsewhere, and the other three Roosevelts in Europe, was all-consuming. They were sluggish, unable to think about anything except the unknown. Which, by its very definition, defies thought. That all in the family shared the feeling brought comfort to none.

Then, on a Saturday, four days after Thompson had appeared with the censored telegram, the Germans announced that the former president's son was a casualty of war. The report had been broadcast in Berlin and, thanks again to Thompson, a handwritten translation was in the Roosevelts' hands within hours. The last two paragraphs, which finally identified the victim, read as follows:

His pocket case showed him to be Lieut. Quentin Roosevelt of the Aviation section of the U.S.A. The personal belongings of the fallen airman are being carefully kept with a view of sending them later to his relatives.

The earthly remains of the brave young airman were buried with military honors by the German airmen near where he fell.

Again, not the German way. But this, after all, was a Roosevelt.

Later in the day, official notice came from President Wilson, whose note of condolence stated, in part, that Quentin "died serving his country and died with fine gallantry. I am deeply grieved that his service should come to this tragic end."

Roosevelt replied as quickly as he could. It was what one did when he heard from the President of the United States in a situation like this, even though he had so belittled the two men who had held the office since he had. But this was not politics; this was personal. He thanked Wilson for his "courtesy, kindness, sympathy and 'approval of my son's conduct.' "

By the following day, Theodore had steeled himself to write the saddest letter of his life, to Kermit in France. "On Tuesday," he told him, "the first rumors of Quentin's death came; the final and definite announcement that he was killed and not captured came yesterday, Saturday, afternoon. . . . There is not much to say. No man could have died in finer or more gallant fashion; and our pride equals our sorrow — each is limited only by the other. It is dreadful that the young should die . . . but after all how infinitely better death is than life purchased on unworthy terms."

The last two sentences to Kermit were a prelude to the only public statement Roosevelt would ever issue about his son's death. To the newspapers he wrote, "Quentin's mother and I are very glad that he got to the front and had a chance to render some service to his country, and to show the stuff that was in him before his fate befell him."

He had cried, had cried on and off since the moment Thompson had paid his second call. But his tears fell gently; he had not yet fallen apart, not yet given in to the new and impossible reality of his life. That was still to come.

Thompson paid another call the following day, Sunday, but did not knock at the door, merely made himself visible several feet from the porch, shuffling around the circular driveway in case one of the Roosevelts wished to address the press personally. He did not yet know that Roosevelt's brief statement, delivered by mail and thus not yet having arrived at any press outlets, would be the family's only comment for the papers.

At one point, Edith came out to see him. Other than her husband, he was the only human being nearby. She approached him slowly, looked at him through watery eyes, and pleaded with him on Theodore's behalf. "We must do everything we can to help him," she said to Thompson, unable to stifle her tears. "The burden must not rest entirely on his shoulders."

The reporter did not know what to say.

Edith lifted her skirt from the ground and ran into the house.

Having previously promised to address a

political convention a couple of days after Quentin's death, Roosevelt forced himself to keep the commitment. His speech was brief and in some places passionate. Perhaps, at least in part, it was improvised. "I have something I want to say to you with all my heart and soul," he told those assembled. "Surely in this great crisis when we are making sacrifices, surely when we are demanding such fealty and idealism on the part of the young men sent abroad to die, surely we have the right to expect an equal idealism in life from the men and women who stay at home. I ask you to see that when those who have gone abroad to risk their lives, to give their lives, when those of them who live come home, that they shall come to a nation of which they can be proud."

He thanked the delegates for their attention and walked quickly off the stage to applause more dignified than thunderous. Something in him wanted to think only about his boys who still lived, and whom he prayed would continue to live. Something in him wanted to forget about Quentin, forget about what no longer was, what never would be.

It was, of course, impossible. And one of the ways Roosevelt acknowledged the fact involved a charcoal portrait of Quentin as a boy of about ten years old with an angelic expression on his face and golden hair resting above it. The picture now hangs in his father's dressing room. No one seems to know whether it also hung there as far back as 1918, where Theodore could see it every morning as he prepared himself for days he did not want to endure.

Soon the extended family arrived at the manse, as did more mail than Roosevelt had ever received before, even after the Spanish-American War, even as president. It came from friends and relatives and strangers, from people who knew his son or had heard of him or hadn't known he even had a son until now but had respected the father for so many years that they had to express their grief; it came from the man on the street in small-town America and from the most esteemed of his countrymen and foreign statesmen; it came from rich and poor, black and white, from Republican and Democrat, warmonger and pacifist, from hunter and even, in a few cases, from animal-rights advocates.

General Pershing, who had refused Roosevelt's offer to engage the enemy himself, expressed his sorrow at how Quentin's engagement ended. But he "died as he had lived and served," Pershing wrote, "nobly and unselfishly; in the full strength and vigor of his youth, fighting the enemy in clean combat. You may well be proud of your gift to the nation in his supreme sacrifice."

From one of Quentin's fellow soldiers: "It is needless for me to say that Quentin's loss was mourned by everybody in the group. He was one of the most popular officers in the organization, being liked by everyone, officers and men. I know of no one who really enjoyed life more than he did."

To Edith, whom her husband feared would for the rest of her life "walk in the shadow," another of Quentin's squadron mates wrote: "A mother doesn't need to be told the kind of a man that her boy is, and yet perhaps it would make you just a bit happier should I tell you what his friends thot of him, what a regular lad he was. I'd have written sooner but was a prisoner since July 5th and just arrived home a while ago."

And to both parents, from one more of the men who served with Quentin: "The last time I saw him he was doing acrobatics against the moon at night, a feat which requires more than ordinary courage. I left the field before he landed, and had no chance to congratulate him on his performance, but I thought you would like to know of it as it was typical of the young officer I knew — as light heartedly courageous as any man I have ever known."

Others who knew Quentin, not wanting to seem presumptuous or not knowing how to reach the family, did not share their memories of him with the Roosevelts, but with friends of their own. One such memory belonged to W. H. Crawford, who had finished a tour of duty with Quentin's squadron early on, then became the president of Allegheny College in western Pennsylvania. "Our truck broke down," Crawford wrote to a friend who had never encountered Quentin, "and I was too late for the mess, but Lieut. Roosevelt came to see me in the hut, and we had a most interesting interview. It was a wretchedly sloppy night, the lieutenant's rain coat was pretty well spattered with mud, but he was bright, eager and full of life. As we went out into the rain to his sidecar, I said to him: 'Lieutenant, there are large numbers of Americans who are very proud of the way the four sons of Theodore Roosevelt are acquitting themselves in this war.' I shall never forget how his face lighted up as he made reply: 'Well, you know it's rather up to us to practice what father preaches.'"

There were also those who could not confine their feelings to prose. One of them lived in a place called Bismarck, Pennsylvania, which had already voted to change its name. The following appears, unattributed, in a collection of letters and reminiscences edited by Kermit three years later:

> Quentin, young Quentin Roosevelt
> Has a town called after him!
> Some way, as we read the word
> It makes the eyes grow dim.
> How brave they were, how young they
>   were!
> Our boys who went to die!
> Children who played in field and street
> So short a time gone by.
> But romping children here, through years
> Secured from horrors grim,
> Will speak the name of Quentin
> In the town called after him.

The letters kept coming, bundles of them, boxes; in time the volume tapered off, but expressions of condolence arrived at Sagamore Hill for years. They all said essentially the same thing, all came from people who knew the same young man, if in so many different ways. In 1921, Edith heard from a stranger named Lucinda de L. Templin, who worked in the office of the Dean of Linden-wood College in St. Charles, Missouri. "I . . . want to tell you," she said, "that I was a student in Harvard University the summer after your son was killed in France and happened to have the rooms he had there. All of the persons employed on the place — even the maids in the building — spoke of him as if they had lost a personal friend. As they all expressed it, 'He was a regular fellow.' It is really very unusual for a person to be so universally loved by all classes of persons, and yet I suppose they were right when they said of him 'He was his father's own son!' "

That was three years after he died. By then, the Roosevelts had begun to receive souvenirs in addition to messages: a book that had been found in the wreckage, Quentin's leather flying helmet, small pieces of the wooden plane he flew, even the axle, which Theodore and Edith displayed in the North Room. The latter seems a bit macabre, but was apparently in keeping with lingering Edwardian values, a memorial to the departed because it played a part in his death.

Even twenty years later, Edith received a note from a newspaper correspondent, a man who was normally "as direct and impersonal as a surgeon," and she read this judgment: "They speak of Lincoln as a man for the ages; if that be accepted, then Quentin Roosevelt was a boy for the ages — a boy who was a man in the beginning, a man who was a boy at the end."

3

Theodore and Edith Roosevelt, "harried by their grief, by memories of Quentin with which Sagamore was saturated, and by the press," which had finally begun to gather outside in large numbers, left home and moved in for a time with Ethel and her family. She was pleased that her mother and father had chosen her house for an escape, but the visit only made things worse for them. The Derbys lived in a place called Dark Harbor, Maine, and the name could not have better suited the ambience. Theodore began to take "long, lonely walks, his face puffy from weeping." He would return with his tears dried, trying not to alarm Edith, but unable to speak for a while. He tried reading; his eyes would not attach to the page. Edith did not even try. For the most part, she sat quietly with nothing in focus, keeping her thoughts to herself, although it is probably fair to say that she did not think so much as feel, sink into feelings so deep they were reminiscent of hypnosis.

As Ethel's children, too young to understand their grandparents' grief, romped through the house with their usual playfulness, they brought solace at some times, jangled nerves at others. When, in their youthful, innocent voices, they would suddenly break into song, it was Quentin's voice that Edith heard, and she would rise with a forced smile and leave the room. Try as he might, Theodore could not get any comfort from his grandchildren; he, too, would excuse himself after a few minutes of their frolicsome presence.

The Roosevelts stayed with Ethel and her husband for two weeks. When they returned to Sagamore, they found that, despite the fact the servants had remained in their absence, performing their daily chores, the place seemed to have been unoccupied for months. It was well kept up, but musty nonetheless; it was dark, but felt darker; it was quiet, but so much so that it felt lifeless. Edith opened some windows; Theodore simply glanced around, as if the setting were somehow unfamiliar.

And then they saw them. They had been neatly placed on a table near the front door, a small stack: Quentin's last letters home,

319

messages from the grave. It took every ounce of Theodore's strength to open them, and it is not certain that he opened them all. In one of them, their boy told his parents that he was "very proud and happy to be at the front, and would not for any consideration have been anywhere else."

But the front had killed him.

Much larger piles of mail awaited the Roosevelts elsewhere in the house, and Theodore, more than Edith, took it upon himself to answer as much of it as he could, dictating his responses. But he did so "in a voice choked with emotion and with the tears rolling down his cheeks." The effort must have been enervating, so much so that he told his friends that they were not to mention Quentin's name in conversation with him. It was too much, all of it, simply too much.

When some acquaintances came to call on Roosevelt around this time and found both the study and the rest of the house empty, they were surprised. They didn't think Theodore was up to going anywhere. They called his name, searched all the floors of the manse, but without luck. Nor was Edith to be found; the housekeepers did not know the whereabouts of either. Something was wrong.

Theodore's visitors strolled the grounds, walked around the veranda, the area near the windmill. No sign of him anywhere.

Finally they tried the stable, and it was there that they discovered him, his arms around the neck of Quentin's horse — tears, ever-falling tears, streaking his face and dripping off his chin. He did not acknowledge his guests for a while; rather, he kept embracing the horse. Eventually raised his head, said hello, but could manage little more. Soon he was alone again. He might not have noticed.

When it learned of Quentin's death, the French government awarded him the Croix de Guerre with Palm, and hastily constructed a tombstone at the crash site, bordered by rocks neatly arranged in a rectangle. The inscription referred to Quentin as an excellent pilot, courageous and devoted, a man who had been killed gloriously. Later, some of the Frenchmen who had so wanted a Roosevelt Division made contact with Theodore. They asked that he send a message to the people of France, who had always found the grand American family an inspiration. He declined. "I have no message for France; I have already given her the best I had."

4

The war officially ended four months after Quentin's life did, on November 11, 1918. For a time, Flora would continue visiting, "comforting and seeking comfort." Theodore could not accept the former, could not provide the latter. All he could do was "earnestly hope that time will be very merciful to her, and that in a few years she will keep Quentin only as a loving memory of her golden youth, as the lover of her golden dawn, and that she will find happiness with another good and fine man."

After a while, Flora's appearances at Sagamore Hill became less frequent. She spent a few weeks serving as Roosevelt's assistant, helping him with his correspondence and the various forms of busy work he had devised for himself, but their proximity to each other was too uncomfortable for them both. Inevitably, it had to end. Her departure was a gradual one, and after it was complete she wrote a letter once in a while to the couple she had so wanted to be her in-laws. Inevitably, these too trickled off. She simply could think of nothing more to say to this man and woman who had meant so much to her and now, through the cruelest of circumstance, were no longer part of her life. She had no choice but to hope that Quentin's father was right about time's mercies. For her "in-laws" as well as for her.

In time, although too much of it, Quentin's Fouf found herself a good and fine man and married him. There was no further contact of note with the Roosevelts. Only memories.

But long before this, Theodore had fallen apart, finally fallen apart, and there was nothing that Edith or anyone else could do about it.

Roosevelt had declared, in the death notice he had written to Kermit, that his pride equaled his sorrow. It did not. His sorrow — "proud sorrow," the *New York Times* called it, as if there could possibly be such a thing — overwhelmed all other emotions, and would continue to do so. Theodore's friend and earliest biographer, William Roscoe Thayer, saw the deterioration of the old Rough Rider closeup, spending as much time with him as he would permit and almost surely more than anyone else. Thayer could sense not only the shroud under which Edith walked, but another, even blacker, that had descended over Roosevelt, a perfect fit, as if it had been tailored for him, a shroud he would wear for the rest of his days, of which there would not be many. And during which he would wrestle with an emotion he had never known before.

"To feel that one has inspired a boy to conduct that has resulted in his death, has a pretty serious side for a father." It was an admission of guilt, or as close to such a thing as Roosevelt could make, and never had he envisioned that he would know or give voice to such a thing. But he immediately followed by saying that "at the same time I would not have cared for my boys and they would not have cared for me if our relations had not been just along that line." The statement, though, is a dubious one. Many were, and are, the fathers who care for their boys, and whose boys care for them, without the boys being raised in an atmosphere that so idealizes warfare, and the slaying of animals as much as men. Theodore's example, his most fervent beliefs, had been carried to the grave by his youngest son, his Quenty-quee.

And somewhere, deep inside, Roosevelt felt it by now. Thayer would write of him that "he never got over Quentin's loss. No doubt he often asked, in silence, why he, whose sands were nearly run, had not been taken and the youth, who had a lifetime to look forward to, had not been spared."

There was no denying it, Thayer continued. "Quentin's death broke his father's spirit. His friend Hermann Hagedorn, who saw him the very day he heard about Quentin's death, noted in his diary that suddenly the boy in Roosevelt had died. From then on until the end of his life — so Roosevelt confessed to another friend — keeping up the fight was a constant effort. . . . The days of exuberance had gone, life became heavy; his own Great Adventure was closing."

Roosevelt did not want to admit it, not to others nor even to himself, but given his age and the nature of this particular grief, he was powerless. It was the first time he had known such a feeling since his childhood asthma, when he lacked even the power to blow out his bedside candle. He might have "scorned" the work of esteemed novelist Edith Wharton, a distant cousin of his wife's; he might have found her sensibilities too delicate for an old soldier like himself — but for some reason he chose her to reveal the truth of his emotions. He was unable to write about his son, he said, "for I should break down if I tried. His death is heartbreaking."

To others he did not have to reveal the truth. Edith knew that Quentin's passing was a death knell for her husband, and his sons, still fighting the war to end all wars, feared that such a fate awaited the man they loved more than any other. As for Ethel, who had nursed her father back to health after his return from South America, it is reasonable to assume that the tears she cried so frequently were for her father as well as for his Golden Lad.

Theodore's health continued to fail, his weight to drop as precipitously as his spirits. Nonetheless, it was accepted by those in the know that the 1920 Republican presidential nomination was his for the asking. Friends and political associates alike made the pilgrimage to Sagamore Hill to assure themselves he was aware of his standing. Some suggested that a campaign, one that would certainly result in his being back in the White House, feeling purposeful and powerful again, would be the best tonic for him. He listened, but didn't hear. "I am indifferent to the subject," he said. "Since Quentin's death, the world seems to have shut down upon me."

Roosevelt had carried on after losing his father. He had carried on after losing his first wife and mother on the same day. He had carried on after losing his brother, the one he had ostensibly tried to replace with Taft. He could not go on after this. For Quentin's death was not just another loss: it was *the* loss, the ultimate tragedy for Theodore Roosevelt, an occurrence that called into question everything for which he had stood in his life. Even through his sorrow, he must have been aware of the irony, the brutality of it: the old warrior had finally gotten his war, and despite not participating in it, it had destroyed him almost as it had destroyed his favorite child.

Quentin's remains were never brought home from France. Eventually they were moved from the site of the wreck and the crude memorial erected there to the United States Military Cemetery, Colville-sur-Mer, Omaha Beach, Normandy. Many years later, his brother Ted, one of the leaders of the charge onto Utah Beach in World War II, would be laid to rest beside him. This after a life of accomplishment and honor that had lasted three times as long as his brother's.

In Oyster Bay, in the graveyard where Theodore and Edith would reside, near the maples, the oaks, the long-stalked daisies, there is a plaque affixed to the earth in their youngest son's honor. It reads:

Quentin Roosevelt
born November 19, 1897
fell July 14, 1918
He has outsoared the shadow
of our night

Epilogue:
The Lion Departs

Theodore Roosevelt did not die the glorious death of a soldier, as he had envisioned as a child, peeking into the abyss. Far from it. Instead, he passed away in his sleep at Sagamore Hill on January 6, 1919, less than half a year after Quentin had been the one to die in glory.

He was, as he always had known he would be, sixty years old. To be exact, he lived sixty years, two months, and ten days.

The cause of his final ailment, fittingly, for someone whose heart had been shattered, was a heart attack, caused by a blood clot. It had been preceded, however, by two and a half years of suffering from a variety of other ailments: insomnia, a return of his childhood asthma, an infected ear, a recurrence of pain in his leg, and a more mysterious malady, which made him listless and weak and was probably the result of microscopic creatures that remained in his body

329

from the malaria he contracted in the Amazon. All of these infirmities seemed to strike and re-strike him during the Great War, and when Quentin was shot out of the skies they reached the point of no return.

Archie, now the youngest living son, cabled the news to his brothers and sisters. Five simple words: THE OLD LION IS DEAD. Alice received her telegram in Washington. The news saddened her more than she had expected. She had not seen her father much in his declining years, but had continued to promote his policies, especially his opposition to Wilson's proposal for a League of Nations to settle international disputes. She was, in fact, banned from social occasions at Wilson's White House, not just for political reasons, but because she had told a bawdy joke at the chief executive's expense. How Theodore felt about the joke we do not know. But he expressed his gratitude for Alice's stand on the League many times. His daughter by his first wife, long the family's lone outsider, had at last become a Roosevelt.

In 1933, when she published her autobiography *Crowded Hours,* she did not mention her father's passing. Having ignored in print the deaths of so many people who had meant so much in life, Theodore, one supposes, would have understood. His daughter, a Roosevelt indeed.

Family and friends assembled for the funeral, and then later circled the burial site on a day when the winds over Long Island Sound attacked them with damp, icy gusts. They were saddened, but not surprised. They had all seemed to know, at some level of consciousness, that Quentin's death was a harbinger for the paterfamilias.

The minister read a number of prayers. Surely the hardest of them for the Roosevelts to hear was Quentin's favorite: "O Lord, protect us all the day long of this troublous life, until the shadows lengthen and the evening comes, and the busy world is hushed, the fever of life over, and our work done. Then Lord in Thy Mercy grant us a safe lodging and peace at last, through Jesus Christ, our Lord."

Including the prayer was Edith's idea, a final linking of father and son, one that had begun with Quentin's grasp of Theodore's thumb minutes after his birth. She knew that if the boy had survived the war, the old man might have done so too. They might have gone on together — although, to be fair, Theodore was too unhealthy to have gone far. Still, Edith knew how much her husband would have loved to greet his sons upon their return from battle. How much he would love to have shaken their hands, patted their backs, and hugged them while sobbing with pride. Edith herself, of course, would have loved to partake of the same ritual.

And if Quentin had grown into manhood, then middle age, then old age, it is possible that he would have consulted his father's ghost, just as Theodore had consulted Theodore Senior long after he had left the mortal realm behind. Theirs would have been a special relationship, one for the ages, Teedie and Quenty-quee. But it could not happen now.

When all the prayers had been said, all the graveside recitations expressed, the crowd began slowly and reluctantly to break up, the mourners returning to their cars and carriages. It was then, for the first time, that some of them noticed the figure in the background, a large man standing alone, leaning against a tree from where he was barely able to see the old man's final resting place. After a few minutes, he too walked away, trailing the others, "his eyes cast down, watching his footing on the uncertain ground."

It was not the first time he had been in Theodore's company since having relinquished the White House. Some months earlier, after having resumed his correspondence with Roosevelt, he had seen his mentor in a restaurant one night, the first time the two of them had encountered each other in years. William Howard Taft had approached Roosevelt slowly, as other diners turned around and "a sudden hush" fell over the room.

At first, Roosevelt did not see him; he was attacking his meal, paying no attention to anything else. Then he "looked up and saw Taft's tentatively smiling face looming over his table. Immediately throwing down his napkin, he rose, hand extended. They shook hands vigorously and eagerly slapped each other on the back. The other guests applauded, and suddenly realizing they had an audience, the two ex-presidents bowed and smiled." It was, for Taft, the moment of a lifetime.

Their fellow diners cheered. When they stopped, Taft accepted Roosevelt's invitation to join him, and the two men spoke eagerly about the subjects that were safe for them, avoiding those that neither could bear anymore.

Now, though, Taft stood by himself in Youngs Cemetery, Oyster Bay, New York, having said good-bye forever. He had always wanted to be Theodore's friend. He knew for a time that he *was* Theodore's friend. And couldn't Theodore have used a friend, precisely the kind Taft had once been, in the horrible days since Quentin had died? Why did it have to end? Friendship, true friendship, such a rarity in life, if even possible.

In his formal statement about Roosevelt, issued a day or so earlier, President Wilson had praised him for his efforts at breaking up the trusts. He said that Roosevelt "awoke the nation to the dangers of private financial control which lurked in our financial and industrial systems," and that "it was by thus arresting the attention and stimulating the purpose of the country that he opened the way for subsequent necessary and beneficent reforms."

About Roosevelt's attitude toward military matters; about his belief that warfare was the ultimate test of both a man's character and a nation's willingness to come together for the common good; about his having urged the United States to prepare for the Great War far before it did; and about his desire to lead troops into battle at the age of fifty-eight when Americans were finally dispatched abroad — about all of this, Wilson said not a word.

He did, however, posthumously award his adversary with the Congressional Medal of Honor for the bravery he had so long ago displayed in the Spanish-American War.

Further, the president enlisted the armed forces in the country's final tribute to the ex-president. He decreed that all members of the Navy and Marine Corps would wear mourning badges for the next month. He also proclaimed that flags on naval vessels and at Army and Navy bases all over the world would be flown at half-mast from sunrise to sunset on the day of Roosevelt's funeral.

Finally, and traditionally, he ordered that, on the same day, the vessels and bases were to fire their guns every half hour in Theodore Roosevelt's honor.

The guns, as was the case at all such ceremonial occasions, fired blanks.

Quentin Roosevelt, having been shot out of the air by German foes, his body visible in front of the wreckage of his plane.

When the Germans realized their victim was a Roo-sevelt, they behaved extraordinarily, erecting a grave and memorial to him, posing before it with a combination of sadness and respect. **Alamy Images**

ACKNOWLEDGMENTS

It is such an insufficient word. "Acknowl-edgments." As if I felt no special gratitude for the following people, no responsibility other than to make a list of their names, be done with it, and get on to the bibliography. The truth is quite different. I had a very specific idea for this book and it would not have been possible without the men and women whose names are about to follow.

Some of the material in *The Golden Lad* has not been published for almost a century. Some has never been published. Biogra-phers of Theodore Roosevelt have under-standably found the canvas of his life to be a mural of such sweeping proportions that they devoted little space to the relationship between Theodore and Quentin, and to the latter's death and its impact on his father's passing. Thus, in my research, I turned to the dustiest boxes of family letters on the shelves where Theodore's life is catalogued, and read through correspondence that seemed untouched by human hands since it was first filed away.

For this reason, my gratitude goes primarily to two sources. The first is the Theodore Roosevelt Collection at Harvard's Houghton Library. Its former curator, Wallace Dailey, is now deceased, but he and his assistants provided me with access to material for which they had seldom if ever been asked previously. In some cases, they weren't sure where it was, or whether or not it even existed. But they found it, and did so in good spirits and with unfailing ability to answer my questions about it. What they could not immediately discover, they began researching themselves.

Harvard's Widener Library has a smaller vault of Roosevelt treasures, and nicely filled in some holes — in both my manuscript and my thinking.

The second major contributor to my efforts is the Sagamore Hill National Historical Site, managed by the National Park Service. Sagamore is a dwelling that reveals the man as much as any man's home could possibly reveal its occupant, and Ranger Mark Kozoil, oddly known as the museum technician, led me on a tour so extensive that it constituted something of a graduate course in Theodore's life away from public office. It was the Park Service's Amy Verone, curator of Sagamore Hill, who arranged the tour, and Scott Gurney who provided valuable information some time later.

The efforts of Wallace Dailey, Amy Verone, and their staffs enabled me to see virtually every piece of correspondence that Theodore and Quentin had ever exchanged. And Mark combined with some of Amy's assistants to inform me about Quentin's activities in his earliest days in the manse, information handed down from one generation of caretakers to the next, the Sagamore lore. Without these people, no book — that simple.

Dianne Wildman accompanied me to both Harvard and Sagamore Hill, and enthusiastically helped me search the archives, turning up numerous letters from father to son and vice versa. I thank her for that.

As usual, the reference staff of the Westport Public Library in Westport, Connecticut, the finest and most congenial institution of its size in the country, was invaluable in digging out arcane information for me. One example will suffice: in my personal library, I have eight biographies of Theodore Roosevelt. Seven of them do not even list Earle Looker's firsthand account of the White House Gang in their indices; the eighth cites the book but provides no examples of the Gang's behavior in its text. Looker's memoir of his youthful partners in crime was, therefore, the next best thing to a primary resource. For my purposes, the book was indispensable.

Without the library's Debbie Celia, I might not have even known it existed.

My appreciation also goes to Susan Madeo, who arranged to track down not only Looker's volume, but several others through the process of interlibrary loan. Sylvia Schulman, Caryn Freedman, and Cristina Bernardi also made my writing days easier. In addition, I thank the library's former chief executive, the effervescent Maxine Bleiweis.

My agent, Don Fehr, supported the book from the moment I told him my idea, and brought it to the right publisher, Jessica Case, who is blessed with the right assistant, Iris Blasi. From the best to the best to the best. And the same adjective applies to Maria Fernandez, for her design of the book.

Finally, I express my gratitude to Toby Burns, Cailin Burns, and her husband Martin Gunarrson — two golden lads, one golden lassie. Just knowing they were there for me brought sunshine through a lot of storms.

BIBLIOGRAPHY

Collected Works and Archival Material

HC *Harvard College Class of 1919, Secretary's Second Report,* May, 1923, privately printed for the class.

LTR *The Letters of Theodore Roosevelt, Volumes IV, V, and VI,* selected and edited by Elting E. Morison. Cambridge, Massachusetts: Harvard University Press, 1952.

QR *Quentin Roosevelt: A Sketch With Letters,* edited by Kermit Roosevelt. New York: Charles Scribner's Sons, 1921.

SH *Sagamore Hill National Historic Site, National Park Service, Quentin Roosevelt Archives,* Oyster Bay, New York.

TRC *The Theodore Roosevelt Collection, Houghton Library, Harvard University,* Cambridge, MA. (Unfortunately, the collection has not yet been thoroughly indexed or catalogued; thus references to the specific location of materials are not possible.)

TRCY *Theodore Roosevelt Cyclopedia,* edited by Albert Bushnell Hart and Herbert Ronald Ferleger. New York: Roosevelt Memorial Association, Roosevelt House, 1941.

TRL *Theodore Roosevelt's Letters to His Children,* edited by Joseph Bucklin Bishop. New York: Charles Scribner's Sons, 1919.

WL *War Letters: Extraordinary Correspondence From American Wars,* edited by Andrew Carroll. New York: Scribner, 2001.

Books

Amory, Cleveland. *The Proper Bostonians.* New York: E. P. Dutton, 1947.

Anderson, Judith Icke. *William Howard Taft: An Intimate History.* New York: W. W. Norton, 1981.

Auchincloss, Louis. *Theodore Roosevelt.* New York: Times Books, 2001.

———, ed. *Theodore Roosevelt: The Rough Riders: An Autobiography.* New York: Literary Classics of the United States, 2004.

Bradley, James. *The Imperial Cruise: A Secret History of Empire and War.* New York: Little, Brown, 2009.

Burns, James MacGregor, and Susan Dunn. *The Three Roosevelts: Patrician Leaders Who Transformed America.* New York: Atlantic Monthly Press, 2001.

Brands, H. W. *TR: The Last Romantic.* New York: BasicBooks, 1997.

Brough, James. *Princess Alice: A Biography of Alice Roosevelt Longworth.* Boston: Little, Brown, 1975.

Cannato, Vincent J. *American Passage: The History of Ellis Island.* New York: Harper, 2009.

Caroli, Betty Boyd. *The Roosevelt Women.* New York: Basic Books, 1998.

Chace, James. *1912: Wilson, Roosevelt, Taft & Debs — The Election That Changed the Country.* New York: Simon and Schuster, 2004.

Churchill, Allen. *The Roosevelts: American Aristocrats.* New York: Harper & Row, 1965.

Collier, Peter, with David Horowitz. *The Roosevelts: An American Saga.* New York: Simon & Schuster, 1994.

Cooper, John Milton, Jr. *The Warrior and the Priest.* Cambridge, Massachusetts: Belknap Press of Harvard University, 1983.

Cordery, Stacy. *Alice: Alice Roosevelt Long-*

worth, from *White House Princess to Washington Power Broker*. New York: Viking, 2007.

Dalton, Kathleen. *Theodore Roosevelt: A Strenuous Life*. New York: Knopf, 2002.

Felsenthal, Carol. *Alice Roosevelt Longworth*. New York: G. P. Putnam's Sons, 1988.

Hagedorn, Hermann. *The Roosevelt Family of Sagamore Hill*. New York: Macmillan, 1954.

——. *Roosevelt in the Bad Lands*. Boston: Houghton Mifflin, 1921.

Jeffers, H. Paul. *Theodore Roosevelt Jr.: The Life of a War Hero*. Novato, California: Presidio, 2002.

Johnson, Paul. *A History of the American People*. New York: HarperCollins, 1997.

Josephson, Matthew. *The Robber Barons: The Great American Capitalists: 1861–1901*. Norwalk, Connecticut: Easton Press, 1987.

Kerr, Joan Paterson. *A Bully Father: Theodore Roosevelt's Letters to His Children*. New York: Random House, 1995.

Lembeck, Harry. *Taking on Theodore Roosevelt: How One Senator Defied the President on Brownsville and Shook American*

Politics. Amherst, New York: Prometheus, 2015.

Looker, Earle. *The White House Gang.* New York: Fleming H. Revell, 1929.

Lorant, Stefan. *The Life and Times of Theodore Roosevelt.* Garden City, New York: Doubleday & Company, 1959.

Lord, Walter. *The Good Years: From 1900 to the First World War.* New York: Harper & Brothers, 1960.

Manners, William. *TR & Will: A Friendship That Split the Republican Party.* New York: Harcourt, Brace & World, 1969.

McCullough, David. *Mornings on Horseback: The Story of an Extraordinary Family, A Vanished Way of Life, and the Unique Child Who Became Theodore Roosevelt.* New York: Simon and Schuster, 1981.

————. *The Path Between the Seas: The Creation of the Panama Canal: 1870–1914.* New York: Simon and Schuster, 1977.

Millard, Candice. *The River of Doubt: Theodore Roosevelt's Darkest Journey.* New York: Doubleday, 2005.

Miller, Nathan. *Theodore Roosevelt: A Life.* New York: William Morrow, 1992.

Morris, Edmund. *Colonel Roosevelt.* New York: Random House, 2010.

————. *The Rise of Theodore Roosevelt.*

New York: Coward, McCann & Geoghegan, 1979.

————. *Theodore Rex.* New York: Random
House, 2001.

Morris, Sylvia Jukes. *Edith Kermit Roosevelt:
Portrait of a First Lady.* New York: Coward,
McCann & Geoghegan, 1980.

O'Toole, Patricia. *When Trumpets Call:
Theodore Roosevelt After the White House.*
New York: Simon & Schuster, 2005.

Renehan, Edward J., Jr. *The Lion's Pride:
Theodore Roosevelt and His Family in
Peace and War.* New York: Oxford Univer-
sity Press, 1998.

Roberts, Sam. *Grand Central: How a Train
Station Transformed America.* New York:
Grand Central, 2013.

Roosevelt, Nicholas. *Theodore Roosevelt:
The Man As I Knew Him.* New York: Dodd,
Mead, 1967.

Roosevelt, Theodore. *African Game Trails:
An Account of the African Wanderings of an
American Hunter-Naturalist.* New York:
Charles Scribner's Sons, 1910.

————. *Hunting Trips of a Ranchman.* Birm-
ingham, Alabama: Palladium Press, 1999.

————. *The Rough Riders and An Autobiography.* New York: Library of America,
2004.

————. *The Winning of the West, Volume Three: The Founding of the Trans-Alleghany Commonwealths, 1784–1790.* New York: G. P. Putnam's Sons, 1894.

Rusch, Noel F. *T.R.: The Story of Theodore Roosevelt and His Influence on Our Times.* New York: Reynala & Company, 1963.

Smith, Page. *The Rise of Industrial America: A People's History of the Post-Reconstruction Era, Volume Six.* New York: McGraw-Hill, 1984.

Stiles, T. J. *The First Tycoon: The Epic Life of Cornelius Vanderbilt.* New York: Knopf, 2009.

Sullivan, Mark. *Our Times: The United States, 1900–1925, V: Over Here.* New York: Charles Scribner's Sons, 1933.

————. *Our Times: The United States, 1900–1925, I: The Turn of the Century.* New York: Charles Scribner's Sons, 1926.

Thayer, William Roscoe. *Theodore Roosevelt: An Intimate Biography.* Boston: Houghton Mifflin, 1919.

Wagenknecht, Edward. *The Seven Worlds of Theodore Roosevelt.* New York: Longmans, Green, 1958.

Ward, Geoffrey C., and Ken Burns. *The Roosevelts: An Intimate Portrait.* New York: Knopf, 2014.

Wead, Doug. *All the President's Children: Triumph and Tragedy in the Lives of the First Families.* New York: Atria, 2003.

NOTES

Introduction: The Grand Dream of a Little Boy

There were times when the boy . . . Dalton, Kathleen Ph.D., *Making Biographical Judgments: Was Theodore Roosevelt a Warmonger?*, Organization of American Historians, http://www.oah.org/pubs/magazine/progressive/Dalton.html [accessed January 23, 2010].

One: The Beginning of the Story

"No national life," quoted in Smith, p. 865.
"was charmed with such manly sentiments," ibid, p. 865.
"Well done, nobly spoken," quoted in ibid, p. 865.
"a supreme test" and "a way for society" and their "cult is non-virility," Dalton, Kathleen, Ph.D. *Making Biographical Judg-*

ments: *Was Theodore Roosevelt a Warmonger?* Organization of American Historians, oah.org/pubs/magazine/progressive/Dalton .html [accessed January 23, 2010].

"Looked at from the standpoint," Roosevelt, *Winning,* p. 42.

"The most ultimately righteous," ibid, p. 45.

"the Baboo kind of statesmanship," quoted in Cooper, Jr., p. 36.

"The birth pangs" and "No man," quoted in Wagenknecht, p. 88.

"a baby's hand," Kerr, p. xx.

"the merriest, jolliest baby," ibid, p. xx.

"Very unexpectedly," Morris, *Rise,* p. 589.

"Edith is doing well," Sylvia Jukes Morris, p. 168.

"To speak with a frankness," Morris, *Rise,* p. 589.

"all things beautiful" and "rifles and children," quoted in Lembeck, p. 78.

"X" and "The light has gone out of my life," quoted in Brands, p. 162.

"a lot of perfectly incompetent doctors," Sylvia Jukes Morris, p. 170.

"holding her hand," Morris, *Rise,* p. 604.

"revealed an abscess near the hip," ibid, p. 604.

"heroically; quiet and even laughing," ibid, p. 170.

"it was a severe operation" and "she is crawling," ibid, p. 170.

"squarish face" and "strong jaw" and "handsomeness that suited her," Brands, p. 197.

"Do not make peace," quoted in Brands, p. 340.

Two: The Heart of the Story

"manliness, decency and good conduct," quoted in Miller, p. 38.

"and as many other maladies" and "First appearing not long" and "They were terrifying," Brands, p. 9.

"He not only took," quoted in http://en.wikipedia.org/wiki/Theodore_Roosevelt.

"Theodore, you have the mind" and "You must make" and "It is hard drudgery," quoted in McCullough, p. 112.

"I'll make my body," quoted in Brands, p. 26.

"began applying to others," Miller, p. 59.

"the blackest day of my life," quoted in Auchincloss, ed., p. 857.

"I felt as if I had been stunned," quoted in Brands, pp. 81-2.

"Could he run the risk of firing?" Morris, *Rise,* p. 38.

"always afterward felt," quoted in Brands, p. 18.

"combined strength and courage," quoted in Thayer, p. 3.

"I have always explained," quoted in Cooper, Jr., p. 284.

"where he swung chest weights," Morris, *Rise,* p. 60.

"For many years," quoted in ibid, p. 61.

"he found he could bring down," McCullough, *Mornings,* p. 120.

"a young artillery captain," Auchincloss, p. 43.

"[t]he flash of his teeth," Brands, p. 281.

"the first great speech," Morris, *Rise,* p. 569.

"All the great masterful races," quoted in ibid, p. 569.

"I have been both astonished," quoted in Brands, p. 342.

"We are near shore now," quoted in Kerr, p. 94.

"a very lovely morning," ibid, p. 97.

"The War of America the Unready," Roosevelt, *Autobiography,* p. 459.

"Some responded with alacrity," Brands, p. 354.

"smoked Yankees," Roosevelt, *Rough Riders,* p. 117.

"all in the spirit of the thing," ibid, p. 107.

"the delighted faces" and "will always stay," ibid, p. 107.

"At this particular time," ibid, p. 116.

"From an early age," http://en.wikipedia .org/wiki/Ethel_Roosevelt_Derby.

"nervous prostration," Brands, p. 336.

"We have been very much worried," ibid, p. 336.

"a jolly naughty whacky baby," quoted in Morris, *Rise,* p. 443.

"a lot of funny little lizards," quoted in ibid, p. 95.

"The Queen of Oyster Bay" and The First Lady of Oyster Bay," quoted in http://en .wikipedia.org.wiki/Ethel_Roosevelt _Derby.

"I do not want to be vain," quoted in Brands, p. 356.

"San Juan was the great day," quoted in ibid, p. 357.

"just reveling in victory and gore," quoted in ibid, p. 356.

"Always I have the longing," quoted in Sylvia Jukes Morris, p. 175.

"great one . . . nevertheless," quoted in Smith, p. 881.

"a boy's first real encounter," Looker, p. 39.

"Step up and see," quoted in ibid, p. 20.

"remarkable for his calmness," ibid, p. 14.

"Remember, I fell on a chair," quoted in ibid, p. 96.

"What a *fine* little bad boy," quoted in

Looker, p. 165.

"boyish and unstable mentality," quoted in Smith, p. 889.

"gushes over war," quoted in ibid, p. 889.

"freakish duplication of his father," Morris, *Rex*, p. 523.

"you are the most unpleasant beast," quoted in Hagedorn, *Roosevelt Family*, p. 109.

"the grip," *LTR, Volume IV*, p. 1107.

"Poor Quentin has a severe cough," *TRC*, 1902.

"Quentin's sickness," *LTR, Volume IV*, p. 741.

"sick in the stomach," *LTR, Volume VI*, p. 1271.

"A friend of the family," Hagedorn, *Roosevelt Family*, p. 251.

"[D]octors administered chloroform," Dalton, p. 199.

"Alice had no playmates," Felsenthal, p. 41,

"a girl to break," Brands, p. 94.

"She was, by every surviving account," McCullough, p. 220.

"a little soft," quoted in O'Toole, p. 35.

"that Quentin didn't hold his own," Wead, p. 96.

"When we got home," *TRL*, p. 69.

"driving Quentin by his suspenders," Ward and Burns, pp. 128-9.

"Quentin is learning to ride," ibid, p. 72.

"Today was Archie's birthday," ibid, p. 29.

"saluting him, bowing to him" and "it wasn't right," quoted in Lord, p. 44.

"Go easy on him, boys," quoted in Miller, p. 348.

"wildman," quoted in Anderson, p. 73.

"Don't any of you realize," quoted in Morris, *Rise,* p. 724.

"For President McKinley," quoted in Sylvia Jukes Morris, p. 221.

"the bride at every wedding," www .fordlibrarymuseum.gov/museum/exhibits/ TR/lovely.htm [accessed November 2, 2009].

"strode triumphant among us," quoted in McCullough, *Path,* pp. 247-8.

"With his feet, his fists," quoted in ibid, p. 905.

"have grown to be big," *TRC,* letter from Edith Roosevelt to her sister Emily, date unknown.

"Dear Father, Please bring" and "Dear Father, It has snowed" and "This pig is sent" and "DEAR FATHER, I HOPE," *TRC,* postcards from Quentin to Theodore, dates unknown.

"Blessed Ted," *TRL,* p. 30.

"Darling Kermit," ibid, p. 37.

"Dear Quenty-quee," *SH,* June 21, 1904.

"The other day," *TRC,* date unknown but

believed to be in the first year or second year of the Roosevelt presidency.

"Blessed Quenty-quee," ibid, June 12, 1904.

"When I went to sleep," ibid, March 12, 1906.

"what day do you come back," ibid, July 30, 1904.

"emely" and following quotes, *TRC,* date unknown but believed to be in the first year or second year of the Roosevelt presidency.

"capable of considerable mischief," Morris, *Rex,* p. 522.

"grotesque faces," ibid, p. 31.

"There was the occasion," Hagedorn, p. 254.

"attack on this building," quoted in Wagenknecht, p. 175.

"been known to drop projectiles," Morris, *Rise,* p. 15.

"After he lighted a lamp," Churchill, p. 214.

"As Quentin and his menagerie," *TRL,* p. 200.

"They look like a Turner sunset," ibid, p. 230.

"If not delivered," quoted in Looker, p. 104.

One of them . . . This information from Auchincloss, *Theodore Roosevelt,* p. 42.

"that we dragged a chair," *SH,* "The White House Gang: The Jolly Chronicle Of a

Crowd of Boys that Numbered Both a President and a President's Son Among its Members," p. 2.

"pulled Quentin out of bed," *LTR, Volume VI,* p. 1004.

"If you capture something really *sporting,*" ibid, p. 1052.

"I don't see what good it does," quoted in Jeffers, p. 41.

"moth-eaten silk artillery pennant," Morris, *Theodore Rex,* p. 522.

"would win the privilege," ibid, p. 522.

"turned on his heel," ibid, p. 523.

"Swollen noses, split lips," Looker, p. 92.

"became interested in," Sylvia Jukes Morris, p. 266.

"Recently I have gone in to play," quoted in Kerr, p. 104.

"Quentin showed promise," *SH,* report card from first grade, June 1904.

"sit side by side" and "How do you get along" and "I don't know what you mean" and "dee-lighted" quoted in Renehan, p. 72.

"His academic performances . . ." Sylvia Jukes Morris, p. 375.

"is wasting time in school" and "Dear Miss Arnold," quoted in "But can one cane a Roosevelt?", *Washington Star,* December 8, 1976.

"Quentin has left school," *LTR, Volume VI,* p. 1473.

"became the country's little boy" and "adored not just," quoted in O'Toole, p. 374.

"Quentin is really beginning," *LTR, Volume VI,* p. 1030.

"I see him occasionally," quoted in http://wapedia.mobi/en/Quentin_Roosevelt.

"Although I like swimming," quoted in ibid, pp. 381-2.

"I cried," quoted in ibid, p. 382.

"a trick of," quoted in Corderey, p. 39.

DOORLOCKED, author's visit to Sagamore Hill, February 5, 2010.

"smoking, drinking," Felsenthal, p. 59.

"Princess Alice," quoted in ibid, p. 59.

"became a regular," quoted in ibid, p. 59.

"I love all these children" and "great fun with them," quoted in McCullough, p. 367.

"if you are old enough," quoted in Kerr, p. 140.

"a solemn, cunning mite," quoted in Brands, p. 382.

"bustling person," quoted in Caroli, p. 193.

"merry, pretty mischief" and "more cunning every day," quoted in Brands, p. 382.

"tickle and grabble," quoted in Dalton, p. 197.

"first on one chubby cheek," quoted in Dalton, p. 168.

"Until Quentin goes to bed," quoted in Morris, *Rex,* p. 521.

"the cleverest," quoted in Sylvia Jukes Morris, p. 233.

"least martial," Morris, *Colonel,* p. 485.

"I am so angry," quoted in Bradley, p. 204.

"Darling Quenty-quee," *LTR, Volume V,* p. 203.

"In no other country," quoted in Josephson, p. 448.

"superhuman stinginess," quoted in Roberts, p. 42.

"I have been insane," quoted in ibid, p. 43.

"malefactors of great wealth," quoted in ibid, p. 448.

"Well, Father, I just saw," *LTR, Volume VI,* p. 916.

"The qualities that make a good soldier," *TRCY,* p. 235.

"made a great bag," quoted in Sylvia Jukes Morris, p. 120.

"eyes sparkling with delight," quoted in McCullough, *Mornings,* p. 120.

"It is four weeks tomorrow," quoted in Sylvia Jukes Morris, p. 120.

"DARLING EDIE" and "dear, dear letters," quoted in ibid, p. 323.

"I have seen," quoted in ibid, p. 323.

"YOUR OWN LOVER," quoted in ibid, p. 324.

"If a war should occur," quoted in Sullivan, *Over Here,* p. 492.

"a sheer pageant of power," Morris, *Rex,* p. 494.

"Time to have a showdown," quoted in ibid, p. 494.

"Did you ever see" and "By George" and "feast, a frolic or a fight," quoted in Miller, p. 481.

"That is the answer," quoted in Morris, *Rex,* p. 549.

"[t]he wise custom," quoted in *New York Times,* November 9, 1904, p. 9.

"tied with his tongue," quoted in Felsenthal, p. 76.

"could not undo with his teeth," quoted in ibid, p. 77.

"New issues are coming up," quoted in Morris, *Rex,* p. 528.

"There is a little hole in my stomach," *LTR, Volume VI,* p. 1084.

"somehow, the old days," Looker, p. 230.

"high-mindedness stood him," Anderson, p. 103.

"Taft became for Roosevelt," Brands, p. 595.

"They are too much alike," quoted in Morris, *Rex,* p. 380.

"You cannot know," quoted in Brands, p. 595.

"Observers were struck," Morris, *Rex,* p. 552.

"By George," quoted in Wagenknecht, p. 19.

"there are no words that can tell," Roosevelt, *Trails,* p. xi.

"Gentlemen, I do not wish you to think," quoted in O'Toole, p. 14.

"very dirty and very triumphant," quoted in Wagenknecht, p. 20.

"I shall not be more than half satisfied," quoted in ibid, p. 45.

"If I followed my impulse," quoted in Manners, pp. 80–1.

"on an observation bench," Morris, *Colonel,* p. 3.

"At one time," Roosevelt, *Trails,* p. 19.

"The track shot across," O'Toole, p. 43.

"enchanted," quoted in ibid, p. 44.

"Sometimes I shot fairly well." Roosevelt, *Trails,* p. 64.

"a bully camera," *SH,* summer, 1909.

"have had a wonderful time here," ibid, 1909.

"Isn't Notre Dame wonderful?", ibid, summer, 1909.

"and said a little prayer," quoted in O'Toole, p. 378.

"The pointed bullet," Roosevelt, *Trails,* p. 514.

"11 elephants," Miller, p. 499.

"We were in hunting grounds," quoted in Morris, *Colonel,* p. 26.

"Latin is awful" and "dull, very dull," *TRC,* 1909.

"in fear & trembling," ibid, 1909.

"[b]ig of brow," ibid, p. 140.

"freakish duplication" and "queer, prudish chivalry," Morris, *Theodore Rex,* p. 523.

"I want to go home!" quoted in Brands, pp. 658–9.

"It is now near a year," quoted in O'Toole, pp. 90–1.

"sham," quoted in Cooper, Jr., p. 154.

"dismissed the treaty," ibid, p. 154.

"believes in war," quoted in ibid, p. 154.

"loses some of its fine edge," quoted in Sylvia Jukes Morris, p. 374.

"Mr. Roosevelt does not understand" quoted in Rusch, p. 266.

"Roosevelt was my closest friend," quoted in ibid, p. 266.

"a fathead" and "a puzzle wit" and "brains less than those," quoted in ibid, p. 267.

"a dangerous egotist" and "demagogue" and "could not tell the truth," quoted in ibid, p. 267.

"to dissolve the unholy alliance," quoted in http://en.wikipedia.org/wiki/Progressive _Party_(United States,_1912).

"Quentin was still boy enough," Morris, *Colonel,* p. 214.

"any man looking for" and "This is my murderer," quoted in Manners, p. 279.

"Stand back! Don't hurt that man!", quoted in Miller, p. 530.

"dull-eyed," and "unmistakable expressionlessness," Morris, *Colonel,* p. 244.

"There is a bullet," quoted in Miller, pp. 530–1.

"to be as quiet as possible," quoted in Lehrman, Lewis E., *The [Stamford, Connecticut] Advocate,* October 21, 2009, p. A-11.

"Take me to where," quoted in Morris, *Colonel,* p. 247.

"with my whole heart and soul," quoted in ibid, p. 531.

"crowded around and tried to slap," ibid, pp. 246–7.

"There is no repentance," quoted in Wagenknecht, p. 202.

"The trip combined," Brands, p. 738.

"kept them at bay," Morris, *Colonel,* p. 291.

"Rounding a little projection," Roosevelt, *Nicholas,* p. 121.

"The skies were the home" and "almost gothic grotesqueness," Brands, p. 740.

"Colonel Roosevelt" and "a bowl of strawberries," quoted in Millard, p. 238.

"A packhorse had slipped," Morris, *Colonel,*
p. 373.

"I don't believe," quoted in Millard, p. 1.

"an affectionate, soft hearted," quoted in
Sylvia Jukes Morris, p. 373.

"Heavens!" quoted in Hagedorn, *Roosevelt
Family,* p. 296.

"What strength is to weakness," quoted in
Amory, p. 315.

"never-to-be-sufficiently-anathematized,"
quoted in O'Toole, p. 375.

"not fine reading," quoted in ibid, p. 375.

"disapproved of me strenuously," quoted in
ibid, p. 375.

"There are far too many black marks," *SH,*
October 23, 1909.

"Only fair," ibid, February 6, 1915.

"I'm awfully afraid," ibid, November 15,
1912.

"Excellent indeed," ibid, October 22, 1910.

"literary correspondent," Morris, *Colonel,*
p. 439.

"I am very glad" and "You are all right,"
TRC, September 29, 1913.

"tended to churn out," Renehan, p. 80.

"The other day we were discussing," *TRL,*
pp. 160–1.

"almost drowned," Renehan, pp. 80–1.

Three: The Soul of the Story

"the Austrian ultimatum to Serbia," Johnson, p. 642.

"the primal tragedy," ibid, p. 642.

"If I had been President," quoted in Lorant, p. 593.

"The storm that is raging in Europe," Cooper, Jr., p. 284.

"The situation in Europe," *TRC,* August 2, 1914.

"no man could buy a substitute," quoted in Cooper, Jr., p. 406n.

"create international conditions," quoted in Cooper, Jr., p. 279.

"yellow" and "molly-coddle pacifist," quoted in *WL,* 145.

"a timid man, physically," quoted in Cooper, Jr., p. 283.

"neither a gentleman nor a real man," quoted in Sullivan, *Over Here,* p. 493.

"skunk" and "prize jackass," quoted in Morris, *Colonel,* p. 445.

"a wonderful row" and "fine and hearty," quoted in Dalton, p. 480.

"such as the regiment," quoted in Morris, *Colonel,* p. 131.

"a dreaming boy," ibid, p. 493.

"tens of thousands," ibid, p. 493.

"If I am allowed to go," quoted in Burns

and Dunn, p. 152.

"At the present moment," quoted in Sullivan, *Over Here,* p. 497.

"I really think," quoted in Burns and Dunn, p. 152.

"My dear sir," quoted in Morris, *Colonel,* pp. 489–90.

"one tenth," quoted in ibid, p. 490.

"Golden Lads," TRC, February 27, 1918.

"the feeling [of reluctance]," quoted in Brands, p. 786.

"his constitutional weakness," Sylvia Jukes Morris, p. 115.

"How can I work," *SH,* February, 1916.

"His room was strewn," *HC,* p. 28.

"inherited one fortune," O'Toole, p. 375.

"slender, dark-haired," Sylvia Jukes Morris, p. 412.

"I don't see why," *TRC,* 1916.

"take any unnecessary risks," quoted in Morris, *Colonel,* p. 498.

"would not have defrayed," O'Toole, p. 376.

"danced all night," Morris, *Colonel,* p. 463.

"the most adventurous," Wead, p. 97.

"loved heights," Morris, *Rex,* p. 523.

"Look down on the White House," quoted in ibid, p. 523.

"or reclined in a chair," Looker, p. 115.

"We're speed demons," quoted in ibid, p. 218.

"one which can fly," quoted in Manners, p. 300.

"A Trip on an Airship," *TRC,* March 11, 1908.

"I did three hours and a half," *SH,* January 29, 1918.

"Aviation has considerably altered," quoted in *QR,* p. 79.

"poured hot and cold water," Wead, p. 97.

"uniform & appalling dullness," *SH,* August 6, 1917.

"yesterday I succeeded," ibid, August 6, 1917.

"Death, whom I had cursed," quoted in *QR,* pp. 26–7.

"a slacker," quoted in Wead, p. 97.

"In fact, the illness was so bad," Collier and Horowitz, pp. 217–8.

"Dearest Father," *SH,* March 8, 1918.

"the surgeon pried a large chunk," O'Toole, p. 359.

"He is very thin," *QR,* p. 142.

"often managed to annoy," ibid, p. 218.

"Cheers, oh cheers," quoted in O'Toole, p. 375.

"part is one of," quoted in Manners, p. 306.

"thrilled" and "I know well how hard," *TRC,* June 17, 1918.

"We have a real man" and "We boys would do anything," quoted in Hagedorn, *Roo-*

sevelt Family, p. 378.

"All the family," quoted in ibid, p. 378.

"so darling and pretty," *TRC,* July 28, 1919.

"Why don't you write to Flora," quoted in Brands, 792.

"idiotic ruling," quoted in Miller, p. 561.

"I got a lot of letters," *TRC,* November 1, 1917.

"Dearest Mother; —," ibid, June 25, 1918.

"hearty and absolutely square" and "Quentin Roosevelt was," quoted in Wead, p. 97.

"smashed one plane up beautifully," *SH,* March 29, 1918.

"They have been in service," *QR,* p. 125.

"life of a chase pilot," Morris, *Colonel,* p. 527.

"We all went over to the funeral," *QR,* p. 111.

"coup de main," quoted in *QR,* pp. 229–30.

"I was scared," quoted in Morris, *Colonel,* p. 528.

"got cut off by a cloud," *New York Times,* June 19, 1918, p. 13.

"You get so excited," *WL,* p. 145.

"I saw my tracers," ibid, p. 145.

Four: The End of the Story

"dug a grave," O'Toole, pp. 390–1.

"We lost another fellow," *QR,* p. 160.

"Watch Sagamore Hill," quoted in Brands, p. 797.

"had been rehearsing this moment," Brands, p. 798.

"His pocket case," quoted in Morris, *Colonel,* p. 532.

"died serving his country," quoted in Manners, pp. 306–7.

"courtesy, kindness, sympathy," ibid, p. 307.

"On Tuesday, the first rumors," quoted in Brands, p. 800.

"Quentin's mother and I," quoted in Miller, p. 562.

"We must do everything," quoted in Brands, p. 798.

"I have something," quoted in Sullivan, *Over Here,* p. 500.

"died as he had lived," *QR,* pp. 198–9.

"It is needless for me to say," ibid, pp. 211–12.

"walk in the shadow," quoted in Brands, 800.

"A mother doesn't need to be told," *QR,* p. 242.

"The last time I saw him," ibid, p. 246.

"Our truck broke down," ibid, pp. 232–3.

"Quentin, young Quentin Roosevelt," ibid, p. 275.

"I . . . want to tell you," *SH,* August 31, 1921.

"as direct and impersonal," Looker, p. 151.

"They speak of Lincoln," quoted in ibid, p. 151.

"harried by their grief," Renehan, p. 198.

"long, lonely walks," Wead, p. 99.

"very proud and happy," quoted in Manners, p. 307.

"in a voice choked," Wagenknecht, p. 180.

"I have no message," quoted in ibid, p. 180.

"comforting and seeking comfort," O'Toole, p. 393.

"earnestly hope that time," quoted in ibid, p. 393.

"proud sorrow," quoted in New York Times, July 18, 1918, p. 8.

"To feel that one has inspired a boy," quoted in Ward and Burns, p. 210.

"he never got over Quentin's loss," Thayer, pp. 447–8.

"Quentin's death broke his father's spirit," Lorant, p. 614.

"scorned," quoted in Felsenthal, p. 71.

"for I should break down," quoted in Brands, p. 803.

"I am indifferent to the subject," quoted in Morris, Colonel, p. 548.

Epilogue: The Lion Departs

"the old lion is dead," quoted in Miller, 566.

"O Lord, protect us," quoted in Sylvia Jukes Morris, pp. 436–7.

"his eyes cast down," Manners, p. 313.

"a sudden hush," Miller, p. 359.

"looked up and saw," Miller, pp. 359–60.

"awoke the nation" and "it was by thus arresting," quoted in *New York Times,* January 8, 1919, p. 4.

ABOUT THE AUTHOR

Eric Burns is a former correspondent for NBC News and the TODAY Show. For ten years he was the host of the top-rated "Fox News Watch," and he has won an Emmy for media criticism. He is the author of *1920: The Year that Made the Decade Roar, Infamous Scribblers, The Spirits of America,* and *The Smoke of the Gods,* and the latter two were named "Best of the Best" by the American Library Association. Eric lives in Westport, Connecticut.

7/14/16